HOW *WILD* THINGS *ARE*

HOW *WILD* THINGS *ARE*

Analiese Gregory

Narrative text Hilary Burden
Photography Adam Gibson

Hardie Grant

BOOKS

I would like to acknowledge the Traditional Custodians of the land that I walk, live and work on, the Melukerdee People of the South East Nation, and pay my respects to Elders past, present and emerging.

Foraging for seablite and samphire
in Pipe Clay Lagoon, South Arm

Contents

The Docks, Flinders Island

INTRODUCTION

Haute and feral. What makes Analiese Gregory one of the most intriguing chefs of her generation? And is it too much to ask that she wants you to be able to cook like her? Writer Hilary Burden unravels the intrepid chef's life journey.

From a wild childhood growing up in New Zealand to quarantine cooking in an earthy farmhouse in southern Tasmania, via the gruelling rigour of Europe's great kitchens, Franklin Restaurant's award-winning former head chef wants you to know that anyone can be adventurous about cooking – and she shares some of her favourite recipes to prove it.

Even if you're not inclined to self-analysis, ringing in a new year at the start of a new decade makes you rethink everything, and Analiese Gregory has decided she needs to be more relaxed. When she handed in her resignation at Hobart restaurant Franklin, there was no job lined up to go to, but she knew she couldn't keep going the way she was. Living on leftovers. Treating her Tasmanian home like a rural hotel room. Missing her goats, who kept escaping in revolt. She spent Christmas reflecting on how her decade was ending the same way it started, running the movie in her mind, trying to figure out how she managed to find herself, yet again, in such a stressful state of being. The one she moved to Tasmania to escape.

Wind back a month: National Geographic TV's just been in touch. Would she like to accompany global celebrity chef Gordon Ramsay during his visit to Tasmania for his *Uncharted* series this summer? A *Monocle* magazine reporter and photographer have just wound up an interview, portraits, and plate shots – hard flash – inside and out of the farmhouse, with some other shots taken with a 1980s pocket Olympus with Kodak film, which all the hipsters love now, apparently, for a 'how chefs cook at home' series. She is head chef at Franklin Bar & Restaurant five nights a week, so that leaves two days, and at the moment her days off are spent flying: to Brisbane for the Good Food Guide Awards, to Sydney for a cooking class at Carriageworks Farmers' Market, and to Melbourne to see her partner, chef Nick Stanton. She tries to avoid hanging out with chefs, but it's easy because they understand her life.

Meanwhile Hazel, the ageing pet rabbit, Nanny and Fanny, the escaping miniature goats, Luke the rooster, and eleven hens-a-laying all rely on her and the Jimny – her army-green Suzuki 4WD, strewn with diving gear and fishing rods – to rocket back up the gravel track, usually after midnight, navigating down a road with no streetlights or concrete street furniture to guide her. That's why people who have left big city lives move here.

Analiese Gregory needs to be home more.

Home is a 1910 weatherboard farmhouse, once a pig farm formerly known as Broadlands, and, later, a veterinary surgery, just outside the town of Huonville (pop 2714), a 40-minute drive from Hobart. Her immediate neighbours – newly arrived distributors of natural wines who are planting their own vineyard – rescue her goats when they escape and mow her lawn when she's not home, which is often.

After flying back from Brisbane, Analiese falls straight into bed and pulls a fake-fur blanket up under her chin. She feels motivated by the two hats Franklin retained at the Good Food Awards, a reminder she posts on Instagram – just before closing her eyes – to *keep on pushing*.

Dawn mist drifts up the Huon River, winding its tentacles through big swamp gums. The hundred-year-old pear tree in the paddock is just bursting into creamy blossom, and a pair of rosellas sits on the farmgate, watching chooks peck at grain scattered briskly under the bushy old bay tree. The goats are climbing on the trestle table, set up in the garden for lunch if it's not turned cold and rainy by then.

She'd bought the farm on a whim at the height of summer after having no fixed address for a couple of years. She has just endured her first Huon Valley winter, where temperatures rarely lift above fifteen degrees Celsius and are frequently below zero. She says she falls in love with impossible projects. The house is 110 years old, there's an open fireplace in every room and she is managing to keep them stoked and going, sometimes two at a time. The window frames are peeling, the showerhead is one of those handheld ones with a rubber hose, there is no exhaust fan in the kitchen, and the Westinghouse Kimberley oven is a bone of contention.

Who hasn't entertained the romantic notion of buying an acre of land with old sheds and a glasshouse, of being able to stroll across the road down to the river to swim? But the notion is real, and it's nothing new. In this place, it is what people have always done. Tasmanians are accustomed to choosing a slower life, one that is also hard because it relies on the seasons, and growing and making things with your hands, all while holding down a day job that tends to strangle the passions that abundance in the natural world inspires.

Sometimes she wishes she didn't hear the call to take the hard road. Not everyone gets it. Old friends from her chic Sydney days – working at Quay and running her own wine bar, Bar Brosé – have visited. One ventured outside into the paddock and came back inside quick smart because there were bees. 'We were friends in Sydney,' Analiese says.

Clearly the reporter from *Monocle*, sitting at the kitchen table, is wondering why on earth the two-hatted chef she's flown down from Sydney to interview hasn't renovated yet. Analiese stands at the oven, stirring and beating polenta for half an hour with a whisk. She hasn't been around a Westinghouse stove, not since she was a kid living in rented accommodation and her mum cooked on one, 'you know, when people had those aluminium cake tin lids that covered the elements'. She had considered ripping it out and leaving it in the driveway for someone to pick up, but friends told her she was being stupid and reminded her how sometimes she gets carried away. The oven has no racks because she took them out, put them on top of some bricks and cooked with them in the garden until winter came and she was forced to cook inside. On Kimberley.

She eats butter like cheese and walks fast, but at home she cooks slowly, and with ingredients close at hand.

She drives for half an hour on a Sunday to buy fresh produce, harvested from the greenhouse in front of her eyes – anything to avoid a supermarket. Her Jimny is packed with what she considers essential equipment, which travels with her everywhere: dive gear, towel, tent, water bottle, matches, Stanley knife, lantern, two fishing rods. Two stoves: a small, portable camping one and a high-powered wok burner ('brand-named "Rambo", I didn't call it that'). And a wok that really badly needs seasoning at the moment because she left it outside.

The glove box is like an overnight bag. Before moving here, she'd spent enough time in Tasmania to know there are lots of times you go somewhere and then just don't go home. Not because of the kind of three-day bender you'd go on in Sydney, or Paris or London, where she has also lived, but because everyone has a spare bedroom. And when you've been drinking, or it's dusk or dawn and driving home means you might hit wallabies, possums, devils or wombats, and you would shudder to be the one to turn them into roadkill, a Tasmanian will offer you a place to stay. All you have to do is be open to it.

'I've had some really beautiful weekends and some great times that way.'

On the passenger seat something that looks and smells like a Chinese takeaway, something not pretty, is wrapped up in paper towel absorbing oil. XO sauce, and all the things it is and can be when you are used to mentally tasting ingredients that come from right now – this moment, what you are and where you are at, this precise minute in your life. The fact that you've just got off the plane from Sydney and have driven home without going to the shops because you had to get back to get wood in, light the fire and feed the goats ... and brought the XO sauce you made in the cooking class at Carriageworks with you. You knew how simple and good it would be with some of the eggs the girls laid while you were away, and the tender abalone from Bruny Island you must remember to give time to defrost from your freezer. So good it sat on your lap on the plane home.

The way she packs the Jimny was inspired by her friend Adam James, who took her abalone diving at Fortescue Bay more or less the first time they met. Packed in the back of his car: a wok, utensils, chopsticks, linen napkins and a picnic basket with handmade ceramic Japanese plates, some soy and oil, and a whole range of dried and fermented condiments (fish sauces, abalone salts, pickled jalapeño and misos), because that's what he does for a living.

'We didn't get any abalone, so we never actually managed to get these things out of the car, but I was so impressed because this guy was really living. You're going to go abalone diving, but the fact that you can get out of the water, cut up an abalone, put it in your wok burner and then eat it off a decent plate with nice chopsticks and with all the condiments you might have at home ... That's my kind of proper Tasmanian living, a sign that you're having a really good day.'

In Huonville, where there's still an internet lounge with vinyl chairs and hanging pot plants, no one knows where Franklin is. The restaurant that chef David Moyle first put on the Australian culinary map, and where Analiese came to be, or hide. They don't know and don't care. Most people who live here would say they go to town – by which they mean the city of Hobart – maybe once a month. She goes to Hobart every day. The 40-minute drive is time to get her head together, time to be mentally ready for the rapid-repeat questions that hit her as soon as she gets in the restaurant door. They're easier to handle if she's had some quiet time.

This is a small island, and one where you can hide from the world. Many people do. But with all this success, I wonder what it is that Analiese is hiding from. How is it that she was always gunning to work at a Michelin? A girl from suburban Auckland, a picky eater who survived on Milo, ice cream and lettuce leaves, and left school at fifteen because she was clever enough. How did she come to work alongside some of the world's best chefs, yet now, twenty years after she caught that plane from Auckland to London, now ...

Now she's not doing fine dining. Not forever, she adds ... just for now.

Clarissa, the interviewer from *Monocle*, asks Analiese how she develops dishes, and the chef explains the way her thinking is going for lunch today: 'I thought maybe I'd get a chicken and grill it over coals ... with last night's leftover polenta made with half buckwheat ... but Hilary turned up with East Coast scallops so I think I'll pan-fry them ... somehow work in the cooking class XO sauce ... I might make a sauce out of the sobrasada [fermenting sausage meat she hangs in her wardrobe] ... then depends on how much asparagus I can get ...'

Maybe it's not quite the answer *Monocle* wanted, but it is THE answer.

Analiese wants everyone to eat well at home and doesn't understand why people don't seem to realise how easy it can be. But then, her bread and butter is extreme quality of product, measured and calculated for a perfect moment with impeccably calm choreography, cutting things into little shapes, picking them up with tweezers and cooking them really precisely, within a tenth of a degree.

Quay has been one of the top 50 restaurants in the world for a decade, won Restaurant of the Year on numerous occasions, and has earned three chefs hats for eighteen consecutive years. Analiese worked alongside executive chef Peter Gilmore for five years, when working days were galactic: sixteen hours the norm. At twenty-four she was managing a team of thirty people she had never been properly trained to manage, but she did it because that was what was expected of fine dining chefs.

Her last day at Quay started relatively harmless. Analiese was woken by a message from someone texting in sick. Then came another. Then another from a close friend, a chef and colleague, to say she was resigning. Barely awake, she felt the stress level rise in her neck like blood spilling onto the floor, knowing she had to replace two people and another was leaving. Analiese's mind spiralled.

Who am I going to get to replace this section? How am I going to get through the day?

She thought that everything rested on her head to fix and make better. Sometimes she just didn't know how.

She caught the number 311 bus to work and when it came to her stop at Circular Quay her mind was drifting like the clouds above the Opera House sails. What if she didn't go to work? What if she just stayed on this bus and didn't get off? The last of the passengers had left the bus and the driver would soon close the doors, except she was thinking: 'What if I didn't just not go to work? What if I also didn't go back to my life? Became a wanderer, lived on the street, fuck, what if I just threw everything away and signed up to train for a routine accountant's life because ... because I just can't do it anymore?'

Analiese got off the bus and started work as usual in the kitchen at Quay. The immediate priority took over like it always did. Until something really minor happened and she walked into the office and told Peter Gilmore, her mentor and boss, that she was leaving.

Lunch with *Monocle* turns out to be at the table in the orchard: hakurei turnips with XO aioli, buckwheat polenta with scallops from the east coast, first of the season asparagus and fried sobrasada. The recipe gets written at the end, after we've eaten. 'Just a quiet weekend at home' she says, wryly, mostly to herself.

If she has a signature breakfast, it has to be rice and eggs. She loves getting up and putting on the rice cooker while she takes a shower, feeds the animals and collects eggs. And while that sounds prosaic for a chef pushing culinary boundaries in Australia, they will be the silkiest, made fresh from her hens that lay saffron-coloured eggs because she feeds them real food, and the tastiest, flavoured with a delicate sense of salt and soy.

She jokes that she doesn't know if she's really strange or a genius. 'I don't know where the line is.'

And this is her dance.

More than a recipe book, this is Analiese's journey, a homage to a place at the bottom of the world that lured her and took her in: to good food, taking risks, and to knowing that real beauty – the kind of beauty we seek in nature – often comes with struggle.

Sarah, the ISA Brown

Naughty Nanny, the escape artist

Opposite: Blue cheese made by local
Flowerpot cheesemaker Bruce Kemp

After many hours spent diving for greenlip abalone on Flinders Island, Analiese prepares a meal in the remains of the day ...

Freshly dived greenlip abalone,
shucked and cleaned

NEW ZEALAND

There are obvious clues that Analiese's farmhouse lifestyle in Tasmania is no pretence, that she knows what she's doing. Just five months after moving into her farmhouse in Huonville, there's a pair of glass flagons on the front step, filled with wine slops she brings home from Franklin restaurant, busy fermenting into vinegar. There's the raw shock of charcuterie hanging on a fold-out airer in her walk-in wardrobe. And there's the way she opens up the freezer door to show you it is full of zip-locked parcels of abalone. 'Of course I dived for them myself!'

You wouldn't be surprised by any of it, if girls tended to grow up knowing they could dive for their own molluscs like Aboriginal women once did. While Analiese was raised on a dairy farm at Matamata on New Zealand's North Island, in the mythical green pastures of 'Hobbit Country', she was the kind of country girl – more natural than a paddock – who had twenty-one pets and kept a praying mantis nest next to her bed. The eggs hatched and babies in their hundreds spewed everywhere. When her family drove around Australia for two years, it fitted in with who she was, a child besotted with animals of all kinds, camping with kangaroos grazing nearby.

When she was young, she liked to sit in a field, hang out with dairy cows and read them stories. Her mother, Jacqui, is of Chinese and Dutch heritage and left law school to have children. Her stepfather, Andrew, runs a family dairy farm in the middle of New Zealand's North Island. It was an idyllic childhood for her and her older sister, Mailing: riding bikes and horses, swimming in the pool, digging in the garden, having whatever pets they wanted. She was the kind of three-year-old who slept with a dinosaur collection instead of a teddy bear, who loved spiders and wondered why no one else did. For a while she kept a very large pet rock under her pillow, which worried her mother because she thought she might hurt herself on it in the middle of the night. She had calves and a pony she didn't ride much, but she still made him hot bran mash on cold mornings. When the family lived in Cairns, Analiese bred mice and sold them. Jacqui remembers her daughter's room smelling like male mice.

She was always that kid – the weird one who didn't talk, while her sister was the bubbly one who did the talking for you while you did things like crossed the road with no shoes on to talk to two sixty-year-old horticulturalists grafting hibiscus. She credits her parents for her inability to stay in the same place for too long.

While the family circumnavigated Australia, Analiese and Mailing were homeschooled. Jacqui says their education included the whole set of *Bush Tucker Man* videos and the School of Distance.

Analiese's biological father is Mark Gregory, the first New Zealand chef to be awarded both the Master of Culinary Arts by the Royal Academy and France's Meilleur Ouvrier (Master Craftsman) status. He left the family when she was a baby and enjoyed a career spanning two decades in top European kitchens before 'retiring' back to New Zealand, where he now consults professionally. The girls were raised by Andrew, a salt-of-the-earth Kiwi who owns an excavator and earthworks company. He kept the girls grounded. At the age of twelve, her first after-school job was driving a roller for Andrew, for which he paid her six bucks an hour. She learned how to drive a digger, but then she had an accident running the bucket into the side of a church and that was that.

She wanted to study nineteenth-century English literature, but knew she wouldn't last because of how she struggled to be in the same place, focusing on just one thing. She thought she might like to be a car mechanic or a cook, just so she could do something with her hands. So at fifteen, ahead of her age bracket, she signed herself out of the all-girls school she was attending and went to TAFE in Auckland to do a two-year course in Professional Cookery. Her first restaurant job was at ICON in the Museum of New Zealand Te Papa Tongarewa, Wellington. It was the shortest time she would ever spend working in a kitchen – anywhere. Why?

'They were mean to me.'

Imagine this: you're sixteen, straight out of cooking school because you are two years ahead of your age group. You've left home and moved to a cheap bedsit in Wellington, and you have no idea how to make a dish because no one has taught you. You are thrown into the fish section, and instead of being shown what to do you are asked to write a three-page essay on why you portioned the fish incorrectly. You are asked to leave, and you're not sure what that means, so you sit in the door to the car park wondering if you should get back to the kitchen, or even if you still have a job. Is this what it's meant to be like?

Analiese found out that it wasn't, so she left. 'They were the bad old days.'

Once her sister took her to the doctor when they were home alone. Analiese had fallen into a pit of depression, but when the doctor said she needed to be medicated, the teenage sisters ran away.

'I didn't want to be on fucking Prozac and not be myself without knowing what the matter was. I was like fifteen. We just left and ran away.'

Next, a trial at Logan Brown, a well-established fine dining restaurant she loved because of the family vibes, run by Steve and Al, who treated their staff like they were part of the family, taking them on farm visits and to the coast to spend a day on a cray boat. Pāua fritters were Analiese's introduction to abalone, although following Al's interest in diving would come to her much later – in Tasmania.

Still unsure of her path, she enrolled at Victoria University of Wellington to do a BA double major in French and English Literature and was accepted, then hit by a wave of panic, and she didn't turn up on the first day – or any.

'For a long time, I wasn't sure it was the path I had seen myself taking.'

Like many Kiwis who grow up in New Zealand, extremely isolated from the rest of the world, Analiese held a burning desire to leave it. At eighteen, she found herself on the Departures escalator at Auckland airport, realising it was the first time she had seen her mother cry.

TRAVELS

Analiese was eighteen and had only recently arrived in London with her boyfriend when France's most famous chef took his own life. Bernard Loiseau, owner of the Côte d'Or restaurant in Burgundy, was one of only twenty-five chefs in the country holding three Michelin stars. He was fifty-two. The book his death inspired – *Perfectionist Life and Death in Haute Cuisine* by Rudolph Chelminski – is among the many cookbooks stacked in Analiese's hallway library in her house in Tasmania, along with Elizabeth David's *French Provincial Cooking* and Nigella Lawson's *How To Be a Domestic Goddess*.

In the book, Bernard Loiseau is described as a man who devoted all he had to his dream, but ultimately paid with his life for trying too hard to please too many people all the time.

Chelminski goes on to describe that it was more than a shock: it was almost unfathomable, from a man who seemed to have it all, including a luxury hotel and restaurant that held the Michelin guide's highest rating. He seemed on top of his game, but he still chose to end it.

For a long time, France has given the provincial chef the same status as the philosopher and essayist. But the world of the *haute gastronomie française* is a very particular kind of pressure cooker, dating to 1933 when the Michelin Guide began to rate French restaurants of high culinary merit: one star meant 'very good restaurant'; two stars 'worth a detour'; three stars 'exceptional cuisine, worth a special journey'.

At that time, provincial French chefs espoused 'cuisine de terroir', buying most of their ingredients from farms, villages and open-air markets in the immediate vicinity of their restaurants. In the 1950s, Fernand Point at La Pyramide upped the ante with his insistence on cooking to the day's market, cooking it at the last minute, individually for each client, and perfectly.

In considering the chef's obsession with perfection, Chelminski writes how restaurants can be like a calling, and also how, frequently, those following this calling are driven by a desire, a passion, to go above and beyond, to never settle for the bottom line – a trait shared by many artists. Chefs at the top of their game approach the profession and their craft with a sense of utter sincerity.

In the big cities, he says, the pleasure is more centred on the dazzle and flash of novelty, but in a great provincial inn, the restaurant is the centrepiece of a larger whole, an escape for a few hours or days into an enveloping haven of peace and repose.

But peace wasn't part of the scene in early 2000s London, where Gordon Ramsay was everywhere, channelling Hell. Everyone Analiese met advised her not to work with him. Instead, her father's head chef suggested she try out at the boutique Capital Hotel in Knightsbridge, where Eric Chavot, the French Michelin-starred chef from Arcachon in the south of France, ruled over the two-star, twenty-nine-seater restaurant and its eight chefs. It became Analiese's baptism by fire.

Vans returned early on Mondays from the Rungis international food market in Paris with pristine produce wearing tags with their provenance. It was her first taste of foie gras, the first time she prepared or cooked rabbit, or pigeon, or turbot (a big fish from the English Channel), or brown crab from Cornwall, or took a whole saddle of venison out of the cool room and pulled off half onto a chopping board.

'Heaps of things totally blew my mind.'

The good, the bad and the ugly.

The Capital Hotel was highly organised and very clean, and a place where 'okay' was simply not good enough. Anything mediocre was thrown away and had to be made from scratch again. Sometimes to get to the pass you had to walk over broken glass – literally. Kitchen staff drank water out of Hildon water bottles. When the chef got upset, he threw their water bottles onto the floor, smashing them to pieces. Once Analiese had to walk this gauntlet to take a prepared rabbit to the chef, and all she could think was, 'The rabbit had better be the best thing I've ever cooked in my life'. If not, she would get told 'No! Merde!', her spoons thrown to the floor, and she would bend down to pick them up only to hear him say, 'No, don't touch! Leave them!'

But she really liked him, and saying that takes some grit. She says worse things happened, though never to her, and, at a time when women were just not seen in sous chef positions, he promoted on talent.

'That was rare in those days. It shouldn't have been, but it was.'

In London, Analiese loved shopping for fashion, surprising her work colleagues by turning up in civvies that were tutus and flouncy skirts or fur coats and lace nighties. The only flat shoes she owned were her chef's shoes. Vivienne Westwood's shop in World's End, Chelsea, was a favourite haunt. One year she decorated a Christmas tree with sparkly shoes instead of baubles.

If she wasn't already toughened up, leaving home at sixteen, she was well and truly hardened by two years at The Capital, though not quite to the point of tears in the bathroom like some of her peers. That would come later, at Le Meurice, the apogee of luxury hotels in the heart of Paris.

By twenty she had moved to The Ledbury in Notting Hill, a part of West London still basking in the fashionable spotlight of the rom-com movie *Notting Hill*; diving into the deep end she thrived on alongside two-star Michelin chef Brett Graham, the Aussie who moved to London and became Young Chef of the Year in 2002.

Socialising with other chefs, for the first time Analiese realised she was not alone. One chef told her the pressure had once got so much he walked into the street outside the restaurant and thought about jumping in front of a bus.

'These are the horrible things the industry hides because it's all about success. Being vulnerable is never seen as a positive.'

She was seeing the anxiety she had lived with from an early age, worrying about everything – from everyday things to how her parents were going to pay the rent – reflected in the people she least expected: her mentors. She recognised her own peculiar type of high-functioning anxiety that, instead of driving you to spend days under the duvet, drives you to constantly do things all the time, always gunning for excellence. In fact, for someone who had learned to live with anxiety, cooking had become a form of relaxation: 'I don't think when I cook.'

The kitchen at Le Meurice (part of the Dorchester Collection) is vast, taking up the entire ground floor of the palatial hotel. Here, there were tears in the bathroom. Well, not the bathroom. If ever tears were welling she did the loop to the washup, following the line of its conveyor belt to find some piece of equipment that she didn't really need – maybe a lid for a container that she just had to have that split second – then worked her way back to the kitchen, hopefully by that stage having calmed herself down. It was her escape of choice from the victimisation that came with being the only female in the savoury *gastronomic* section and not speaking French. Running off to the bathroom would have made it way too obvious that she had reached breaking point. The highs were as vertiginous as her off-duty designer heels, but she was learning the tricks of the trade. Poker face. Work hard. Show no fear.

Back in Huonville, sipping New Zealand native gin while sitting under woollen blankets in front of the flames of a wood heater, Analiese remembers being at Le Meurice when the hotel won three Michelin stars. Imagine the massive, no-expense-spared party in Les Étoiles, a music club off Les Champs-Élysées, where everyone showered each other with Cristal Champagne, burned through crazy luxury mountains of foie gras and caviar, and best-of-the-best ingredients like lobsters from Brittany and the kind of thick asparagus favoured by Alain Ducasse.

Eventually Analiese was promoted. She moved sections many times as she discovered for herself that the drive for perfection in the Michelin kitchen had devastating costs.

'I always thought that when I was working in a three-star restaurant everything would be perfect. When I was in Paris living my dream and we won three Michelin stars I realised, no, not everything is perfect. Maybe nothing's perfect anywhere.'

Her next thought was: 'Oh my God, what am I even doing with my life?' She was twenty-one.

She didn't want to leave Paris, but her father, Mark Gregory, was opening a hotel in New Zealand and made her executive chef of her own restaurant. Analiese had dreamed about going back, but it felt wrong dancing to her father's tune. She realised he should not be her reason for doing things.

What was it like moving from the 20th arrondissement in Gambetta, where she could shop for food every weekend in the Paris markets, to a beach haven suburban home in Auckland and working for family?

'I'll never do it again.'

Later, she went to work with Peter Gilmore at Quay in Sydney. As pastry chef, she learnt to make his eight-textured chocolate cake, famous for being a three-day process that involved tempering chocolate, as well as being one of the most ridiculous challenges on Australia's *MasterChef*. It was so renowned, in fact, that fans repeatedly asked Analiese how to make it. Being eight separate recipes combined to make one cake, she told them it was a recipe that should never be attempted at home.

They did some weird stuff.

Like? Like Peter wanted to make a sphere out of squid with squid consommé in the centre. So they made squid consommé, turned it into a jelly and wrapped it in squid, then placed it in a bath of clarified butter and tried to cook it, even though only one in ten held together. The rest burst, 'because squid is not a protein that bonds together in that way'.

The whole thing is a level of intensity few chefs attempt. Analiese simply says, 'It's labour intensive'. Peter says she's the best chef to ever come through his kitchen.

He was the most supportive person Analiese had ever worked for, but she never told him she was struggling. Gilmore was shell-shocked when his protégé told him she was leaving.

'You need to calm down,' he implored her. 'You're meant to be running the kitchen, you need to be in control.'

But she wasn't, and she left. At twenty-six, she walked out on what she thought was her forever life.

'When you're like that, you do become really selfish without meaning to because you can't think about anything outside yourself. I had become an angry chef and I didn't like who I was.'

She found she liked herself better in countryside France, where she started another life on her own and could be whoever she wanted. Gone was the city-sider who lived in high heels and never wore flats or jeans. Instead she bought hiking boots and returned to the nature girl she once was in a place where no one knew her, and which seemed a better fit with her New Zealand childhood after all.

'I know it's a bit like running away and your baggage catches up to you eventually, but for a while you have this freedom without any of the baggage of your previous life.'

Immersed in the flowers, the fragrant herbs, your smile, your grace made every day special. Ana, I will always remember your attentiveness, your care to do your best to bring the dishes to life. I wish you a successful career.
Warmest wishes, Michel. Oct 2013.

Michel Bras is a legend. The charming, understated former executive chef at Bras in France's Aubrac region held three Michelin stars from 1999 until 2017, when he voluntarily gave up his rating. He was calm and undemonstrative, and very proud of his academy of trainee chefs and a kitchen where heaven was made and eaten on Earth in the form of Le Gargouillou, his signature salad of fifty-two herbs and edible flowers.

Once a year for many years, Analiese had written a letter to Michel Bras inquiring about working in his kitchen. She wanted to work with the best. Something to do with growing up where she did in New Zealand, with a fear of suburbia and the mediocre. Finally, there came a response from Regis, his head chef. Analiese was at Machu Picchu in Peru with Peter Gilmore, on a trip that had been booked before her dramatic resignation from Quay. It was years since she had spoken French, so Google Translate was the one to explain there was a position available at Bras for the next season, but that they would need to know her answer within a week and that she had to start by a certain date. Her choice was this: to pack it all in and train to be an accountant or work at the Holy Grail of restaurants.

For a year she embraced French country life and it embraced her. She loved foraging, hiking, horse riding, making and drinking elderflower G&Ts, and hooning around the countryside in a bright green Renault Twingo on visits to cheese caves. She adored it all, partly because she felt she had returned to nature, and partly because it reminded her of the New Zealand she had run away from. Where once she couldn't wait to get out, now she saw that what her family had in New Zealand was no worse than the life she was currently living. Working in France with Michel Bras was just a way of redefining it.

'You have to do that full circle or you wouldn't understand.'

She still yearns to be one of those people, like Michel, who grew up in one place and never left, never worked anywhere else. Or like his brother André, who had never even left France.

'We were feeding the cows when I found this out. He looked at me like, "You're the strange one – you've come from New Zealand to feed cows!" It was a good point. To *know* that you love something that much, to know that it's part of what you are and who you are. I'd never had or felt that. I'd grown up in New Zealand. My dad's full Welsh, my mum half Chinese and half Dutch. We were so culturally mixed we had no sense of belonging anywhere.'

What drove her away from New Zealand is the thing that drives her back to those places steeped in the last vestige of what people once had – how humans once lived, and what we seem to be losing faster than ever. Places where you can light a fire on a beach, fish off the rocks, swim in a river, pull a cray, dangle a line, shoot a roo, skin a possum, boil a billy, or just lie on the ground in the pitch dark and see a star world that makes worries vanish.

'I'm a chef because of my anxiety.'

She was just so damn good at covering it up that, even after five years, Peter Gilmore didn't notice.

'I really didn't know I was going to resign the day I resigned from Quay. When I told him, six months later after we'd patched it up, how I was always so anxious and stressed, he told me he had no idea, that I seemed so calm. I realised I've learnt to hide it really well. For all those years in France and London in super high-stress kitchens I learned to walk through it so that other people couldn't tell what was happening. I do that in life as well. In countryside France I had time to do a lot of thinking, talk to my sister about how we are, how people are, how your mind works, and how to deal with anxiety.'

Every morning at six in Laguiole, Analiese joined the Bras staff to pick vegetables for the restaurant. After they'd finished, Ginette, Michel's wife, made *viennoiserie* and coffee for everyone, always remembering precisely how each person would take it. They would gather in the family's home kitchen, embraced by the smell of coffee and warm croissants, Michel's personal collection of vintage whisks hanging overhead. In their sixties, husband and wife appeared happily loved up, but Ginette said that was only because Michel ran twenty-one kilometres a day. That she would not be able to live with him if he did not know how to quiet his mind. Analiese came to see this morning time with Michel as sacred, so hard to come by in the restaurant.

Lessons on how to deal with anxiety may not be what you expect of a cookbook, but it is a story Analiese has considered telling for a really long time – for years. Speaking of it now, sitting at an old-fashioned round table, Analiese is still, like hot milk just before it reaches boiling point.

'You need to know you are not alone, that there are heaps of other people dealing with stress in different ways, people you respect, and it doesn't have to be a negative thing. I always hid it because I thought it would make me weak. I also realise I might not be here doing this if I wasn't an anal perfectionist and had massive anxiety because of that.

'If you have to live with anxiety, you don't have to live with it as a bad thing you need to hide. You can learn to use it for the good that it can bring you while trying to deal with the negative aspects. I don't listen to the voice that says "you're hopeless" ... I listen to the voice that drives me to do interesting things. Changing your mindset about it is probably the most helpful thing I have tried so far.'

It helped her to know that people she respected were beating off similar demons. In France, she learned that she wanted to do the same for other young chefs, offering more than an annual post on social media that you forget about for the rest of the year.

After two years working and travelling in France, Spain and Morocco, responding to the here and now, opportunities arose back in Australia – fine dining in big cities. Momofuku Seiobo with its three hats. Someone suggested she take over the Royal Mail Hotel in Melbourne after Dan Hunter left. But something stopped her. She worried about the soaring reputations those restaurants held, and for some reason that only her demons could see she feared she might be the one to destroy them.

She returned to Sydney because she was meant to be opening a restaurant with her boyfriend, who had waited for her for two years while she travelled to right her mind. They were looking at restaurant sites, writing up business plans, and starting to write menus, but after living the hiking and foraging life, being free in nature, eating really healthily and growing vegetables, an urban apartment in Kings Cross and shopping for dinner at Coles wasn't going to cut it. When her relationship finally ended, Analiese went into a spiral of doom and depression. Why had she left places where she was happy only to come back to this?

That's when she moved to Tasmania, a familiar place she knew through chef and foodie friends, after being offered the job as head chef at Franklin.

Autumn in Tasmania is a wildly
abundant time for mushrooming

TASMANIA

At Gourmet Escape, the annual Western Australian food, wine and music festival where world chefs and gourmands get their taste on for ten days under the bright gaze of the Southern Cross, Analiese was chatting onstage with the head chef of Slovenian restaurant Hiša Franko. In 2017, Ana Roš was named world's best female chef in the World's Best 50 Restaurants, a list commonly associated with Ferran Adrià at El Bulli and René Redzepi at Noma.

It didn't matter much what their live audience thought. Ana and Analiese were having their own conversation in public, Ana tearing into Analiese for wanting to leave Australia and return to France, with its way of life and sense of cooking. Ana told Analiese she owed it to Australia to try and create the thing she was leaving for, because that way of life already existed in Europe. She implored her to go somewhere remote, pick plants, cook and document it. And so the seed was sown between two female chefs in a public moment that would change the course of Analiese's trajectory.

Even when the surface of the sea is rough, life underneath the ocean is calm. All you can hear is the sound of the sea, as if you haven't yet been born. You can be alone inside the womb of your head, in a way that you aren't in the normal world where there is always some outside noise to distract you. Diving in the ocean, you meet a whole other world of creatures and plants totally different to the land world. There are no people, and while it is beautiful, it is also, sometimes, utterly frightening.

Before moving to Tasmania, Analiese had only ever been a holiday diver: 'Look at the pretty fish in the water'. She had never swum in Sydney because she thought it too cold. Now she rarely goes anywhere without a wetsuit, hood, gloves and boots.

How come?

Because Tasmania is beautiful and pristine, and you can dive for luxury ingredients like abalone, wakame or sea urchin with an annual recreational licence that costs very little.

Now Analiese has become so hooked as a diver she says she's renowned among her friends for 'doing stupid things on my own'. Like driving through Geeveston down to the furthest towns, to Dover and Southport, to the southernmost tip of Tasmania, diving off rocks for abalone, or scaling cliffs to collect seaweed to make seaweed jam. Everyone thinks she's taken early retirement, but she works at Franklin five nights a week and her freezer is stacked with her own wild catch.

Some of it is gathered from a week on Tasmania's remote Flinders Island, where she cooked for the Visiting Chef Series with her mate Jo Barrett, baker and chef at Oakridge Winery in the Yarra Valley near Melbourne. When Analiese and Jo took over the kitchen at Flinders Wharf, they did more than cook. They hunted, foraged and dived for their produce. Flinders farmer Mick Grimshaw, who took them diving for crayfish, watched them in the water for hours. He says they bridge the gender divide: 'friggin' legends!'

With two days off, she is heading up the east coast to Dolphin Sands – a place she is drawn to. But first she gets home to Huonville from the restaurant at two thirty in the morning. It was a good night because one of her suppliers – a dairy farmer and his wife – managed to get off the farm and away from the kids to dine at Franklin, where they had never been before.

While most of her customers are international tourists brought to Hobart by the reputation of the Museum of Old and New Art, she says the biggest

VIPs are her growers. How happy it makes her to see them eating her food, especially when it is all about their produce.

She's running a bit late, driving up to Dolphin Sands via Hobart's Farm Gate Market, where one of the growers is pleased to see her snaffle the bunch of white asparagus no one else wanted and place it into her market carry bag along with flowering kale, 'because it was there and looked cute', organic cheese, a bag of green lentils, and a bottle of natural vermentino from the Clare Valley courtesy of her neighbour, who she first met in a very Tasmanian way (one degree of separation): outside Franklin in his role as a wine distributor.

'You don't know me, but I live next door to you,' he said.

'It's just a little bit weird,' says Analiese.

It's been a long drive, three and a half hours, so we head to the nearest vineyard for a late lunch with a view. Chef Zac Green, who lives up the road in Swansea six months of the year and the other half in the south of France, gives Analiese tips on local spots to shore dive for abalone. It is Tasmania. He loves fishing too, and so these two people who've never met before fall into the sort of conversation divers have about sharks and stingrays ... and fear.

'Stingrays are just curious,' Analiese says.

Back at my housesit in Dolphin Sands she starts snapping woody ends off the white asparagus, then looks for a spoon. Thermo plastic, wooden, slotted, a ladle or a spider? When you've been taught the right way, it's hard to let go of needing the correct tool for the job. Luckily, this house seems to have them all.

Like all of her chef friends, she loves being cooked for because she's always the one cooking. But at the moment she's enjoying cooking at home because for a very long time, she didn't.

'I think there's some kind of relationship between how many hours you cook at work and whether you cook at home,' she muses.

For her, there used to be work cooking and home cooking, but lately they've come closer together. Work cooking used to involve tweezers, cutting things into tiny circles, lots of waste, and everything being very precise. At home, she gets ingredients and just goes for it, doing whatever she likes.

'It's a matter of what you have in the house, what's around you, as well as all of the experiences you've had in your life so far.'

She hasn't fully decided what we're having yet. Maybe blanch the asparagus spears first, then pan-fry them. There's a massive bouquet of parsley I picked up in Swansea from the Sunday veggie van. Maybe go with a caper and parsley vinaigrette ... there must be anchovies hiding somewhere.

We drink G&Ts while she raids a stranger's pantry and I ask her where her recipes come from.

'When you look at an ingredient like an abalone or an egg,' she says, 'there are many ways you can cook them. All the ones that come to your mind are things from childhood, your travels from around the world, the things you've done in restaurants. You cycle through a mental catalogue of things, then there's another mental catalogue of things that go with this. Then there's what do you have? Then you look at them and cross reference, and you mentally taste. It's similar, but different, for designers who look at a space and imagine it with furniture. I can look at ingredients and imagine how they're going to taste together. Sometimes you get it wrong, but not very often.'

She says most of her Tasmanian recipes come together this way because it's always about what's around. Michel Bras is in her head too, saying never to buy vegetables from someone you don't know.

What does she take that to mean?

'If you grow something yourself, maybe you can see it from the window of your house; or, if your next door neighbour is growing something, you can picture their family. Then when you go to use that product, a) it means more to you, and b) you're much less likely to waste it or to treat it with disrespect, I guess. You're less likely to throw it in the bin because it's Al's turnip or Al's chicken – it's personal. So, I suppose what he meant is there's a personal connection to those things.'

She's trying to reduce the number of groceries she has to go to town for. Now she has her own chickens, she's crossed eggs off the list. Next it will be honey, but she knows she'll never be completely self-sufficient because she'll always have to buy things like flour. 'At least I can buy it milled yesterday or today by people I like and respect, who are doing something good for the land and the world.'

She's been Skyping with National Geographic, and they'll be here at the end of the month on a three-day reconnaissance for their show *Uncharted*. She's been assigned the role of 'Gordon Ramsay's guide to Tasmania' and they plan to go diving for sea urchin on Bruny Island. How perfectly magical and serendipitous that while she chose not to work for him when she was in London, he is arriving on her patch nearly twenty years later. They talk about filming her walking out of the ocean like Ursula Andress in *Dr No*.

'Yes, I can do that for you, but you do realise I'll be wearing two centimetres of neoprene and a snorkel,' she tells the producer.

For Analiese, uncharted means diving in out-of-the-way spots, where you are under the water and there is no pollution, and everything you see is wild. Wild means taking 4WD-only tracks in a national park and going to places where you don't really see other people. Wild is driving all the way to Ansons Bay to someone's shack on a rough road that makes you think you're never going to get there. Wild is trying to avoid Tassie devils on the road at night and seeing more wildlife than you've ever seen in your life before, even though you're behind the wheel of your car.

Wild can also be feral.

'Like when I go to Bruny and camp on a friend's farm or sleep in his shed and when I wake up I go to the ocean, go for a dive, come back, butcher some wallabies with him, go possum shooting with him, and if he asks, "Have you been floundering?" we go back for waders, and go floundering.'

It is the kind of wild with no real creature comforts that is not unique to Tasmania, but feels more available here than in other places.

We eat pan-fried white asparagus, buttery green lentils and roasted flowering kale with Persian feta and a sharp parsley vinaigrette in a welcoming house that neither of us owns, and we talk about tomorrow: how ideally the water is going to be flat and glassy, and visibility will be really good. She needs to dive. Diving does for Analiese what meditation or yoga does for other chefs who need to control their stress levels.

Analiese would never call herself a good swimmer. She rarely swam growing up and had a fear of deep water, which meant to dive she first had to overcome her dread, along with a hatred of cold water.

'I suppose in moving to Tasmania I mastered some of the fears that had been holding me back in my life, or something.'

It's peaceful in the water, she says again; how really calming it is.

We are rolling about in the Jimny, almost bumping our heads on the roof as Analiese negotiates a 4WD track on the way to Cape Tourville Lighthouse in Freycinet National Park. It's fun, and we hoot and holler and gasp at the ocean blues while Jimny just wants to go faster, the track getting steeper and rougher down to Bluestone Bay. The stones are so perfectly round, and blue like breath on a foggy morning. I ask her what the syringe on her dashboard is for. She says she used it to de-worm the goats before she left home this morning.

She worked in a century-old medina, once, in the city of Fès in Morocco when she was invited to do a two-month chef's residency at Numero 7. She says it has a sense of place as old as the world, that when you look out over the rooftops, with the exception of the satellite dishes, it is like Jesus could be alive and walking around. She says she thought she knew Moroccan food, its tagines and pastillas. It was really the reason she went there. But she found there were other influences: Jewish, Arabic and those of the nomadic Berbers. That's when she realised to really understand Moroccan food, you had to understand the country's migration patterns.

'It became really in-depth and interesting, and suddenly you're in this other world where it's not tagines at all ... it's much more varied and totally different than I ever imagined. People told me about these dishes that became mythical for me – sardine tagines or the monkfish and chickpea tagine that I had in a private home when I first arrived in Marrakesh. It wasn't anything I'd ever seen in a cookbook or ever thought about or had before. It was out of this world.'

When you've worked all over the world and been an angry chef, moving to Tassie seems a reasonable lifestyle choice. Shopping isn't a new dress, new shoes, or a onesie. Shopping is at Tuckerbox for chicken food or goat worming or asking Dallas, the farmer across the road, if you can get three bales of hay from him. You could be back in the medina in Fès, because meeting people who don't know your past is the same in any wild or exotic place: you feel like you can be your best self, not held back by the burden of other people's expectations or the limitations you place on yourself.

You do wild things. In Sydney, Analiese saw her small circle of friends as enough, but in Morocco, she met random people who invited her to their goat farm for the weekend, who drove her halfway across Morocco in a taxi to god knows where.

'I did all of this kind of crazy shit that I could never imagine myself doing. Tasmania is kind of the same.'

Like taking her boyfriend, Nick, possum and wallaby shooting on Bruny Island with a hunter she met through some fishing guys she got talking to in a local pub. 'Have you met Richard?' they asked. She called Richard and he invited her to Bruny for the weekend to go wallaby shooting in the early hours.

'One thing leads to another, and that's what I really like about life, but it seems more possible in places that are wilder or off the beaten track or something. And you have to be open to it – you have to be in a certain kind of mindset and be prepared to have a really unusual day.'

Richard from Bruny became their hunter for Franklin, and his wallaby was on the menu every day. In the beginning, Analiese got a lot of pushback for serving raw wallaby, and she thought she was doing something wrong. From behind the pass she would overhear the upset diner: 'Oh, that's wallaby from Bruny Island ...' They'd been there on the bus and had seen them hopping about the place.

Analiese hadn't been in Hobart long when other local chefs told her she couldn't serve raw wallaby and that she needed to do her research better. She knew Ben Shewry had served raw wallaby at Attica in Melbourne. If he was prepared to do it, she was too.

Now she says attitudes have swung around. Customers want the wallaby dish, and other chefs message her asking for the number of her wallaby hunter.

'Part of it is educating them, and also educating the staff. There's also a shift happening culturally in Australia. You're seeing more anti-beef articles about eating sustainable meat like wallaby and kangaroo ... In Morocco, I'd serve goat because that's what everyone had and that's what was around. I don't like to say it's not about Tasmania, because it is, but for me it's more like a mindset, and you apply the same mindset wherever you are. It's a universal approach to wherever you happen to be.'

Now she is posting pictures of her cooking possum on Instagram, and they're going through the same thing all over again. Why are we so resistant to eating Australia's native produce?

'It's not just the cuteness factor,' she says. 'It's part of how the place was settled, how we don't have a love for wildlife or anything native or associated with the original story – including the people. If it had always been part of the Australian food system, people wouldn't even be questioning it now. It would be common and everyone would be eating it. This is wild game, I suppose, what is of this country. Similar to England during game season when you'll get grouse, pheasant and deer and not think anything of it. It's the same all through Europe. People go and hunt birds. It just makes sense to me that people would hunt wallaby and treat it in a similar way.'

It is taking Australians a long time to get to know themselves. Australia is a colonised country that has resisted being connected to what existed here before.

'It's just that Australia has a weird relationship with Indigenous people. Sometimes cooking that way here, people think I'm trying to bring back Aboriginal food, which I'm not. I'm just trying to cook with what's around me. But I do sometimes feel almost guilty about it because of how everything is over here; how you can be made to feel that you are taking something that doesn't belong to you. In France, you never have that feeling.'

For Analiese's first dive – in mid-winter – the weather could not have been worse. Jack, the sous chef at Franklin, a local boy from Judbury, told her how you could just go down off the rocks to get a feed of abalone. So the two of them drove down to Fossil Cove and Jack, a proper Tassie boy with thighs the size of tree trunks, lent her one of his wetsuits three times too big. It was sleeting, the abs were nowhere to be found, and when they got out of the water she was the coldest she had been in her life. But she was as hooked as a fish.

Nick says when she dives she's like a kid. She knows what he means because when he goes fishing, she thinks he's a big kid too, loving it so much you are excited to get up at four o'clock in the morning. She says she was like a kid driving up the east coast today. Dropping into every little cove to check out the swell, she felt herself go really pouty to see it so big and rough.

Analiese is holding the stem of her wineglass sommelier style: like a pen, between thumb and index finger. She doesn't really praise anything unless it is really, really good. You will never see her chasing peas or lentils around the plate. At the same time, she is arcing right back to a style of home cooking Tasmanians do naturally, like any small community dependent on its own resources.

For many years, being an island state with few restaurants meant that people (mainly women) learned to cook at home, while men learned to cook away from it. Most Tasmanians had a cow or a quince tree in their backyard, or snared possum and shot roo in the bush. Isolated from the city, without a supermarket up the road and with few cafes, life often comes down to brutal or creative self-sufficiency.

Just like New Zealand, Analiese's mother says, Tasmania is like a throwback to everything that is good in life, unspoiled and abundant in plant and animal life – a chef's paradise.

At Bluestone Bay, Analiese parks Jimny at the end of the track, which faces the curved shoreline with its deep teal sea and whitewater waves. She hops out to face it, taking it all in with a calm, intense gaze that is making ten assessments at once about wind and swell and depth, measured against courage and caution. We rock hop in matching Blundstone boots, fossicking for kelp and shells. Her look is made for the front cover of some weekend magazine: a wet-suited mermaid sitting on kelp, catch bag in hand.

It is too rough to dive, but she goes in anyway, inching her bottom over the rounded blue rocks into the whitewashed, windswept swell. She swears it's got bigger since she first got in. She gets rumbled by a set, and after a few more minutes she retreats and sits on the seaweed shore like a gull to catch her breath ... it doesn't matter that the abalone bag she carried into the sea with one hand is empty. She has scratched her itch for a dive and respects what the wild waves are telling her. No abs today.

A text pings in from a farmer. He wants to know if she needs beef.

Her sister, Mailing, who lives in London and food shops at Waitrose, is amazed at how Analiese buys produce. How she'll get six or eight different text messages a day from small producers who might have one thing or twenty, sometimes nothing at all. It's a change of mindset, all to do with what's around, not what you think you want to cook. If you want to know the secret to how to live well in the countryside, this is it.

'People have been collecting stuff around them for hundreds of years,' says Analiese. 'It might be called foraging now, but it's still just collecting stuff.'

While Analiese is a chef travelling at the top of her game, she is responding to a Tasmania where people have always lived and cooked this way, without being photographed doing it. She is giving it much-needed kudos – like good rain bouncing off a long-parched paddock – but resists the kind of attention that turns food into a trend.

'Saying that it's in right now implies that at some stage it will be out.'

People want to put a label on the chef who lives on an island and dives for her own catch, who serves up possum, who forages for mushrooms, but she has never labelled what she does. It is 'farm to table' in the sense that farmers bring in produce that is fresh and seasonal, and the kitchen works with it, doing as little as possible to it. But the approach is not unique to Tasmania.

'Goat's milk, skirret, blackberries, celtuce (originally from China) and seablite are all available somewhere else,' says Analiese. 'Sea urchin and cray are available everywhere. So are pine mushrooms … people think they're niche Tasmanian, but it's really just how you see things. By looking at where you are in a different way, these are things you might find in your environment.'

There's no flag flying in the car park at the Coles Bay tavern where we're sitting at one of those outdoor table and bench sets, sheltering from the strong nor'easterly behind a glass partition. It's lunchtime, but we've resisted the pub counter lunch menu handed to us by a barman who calls you 'buddy' and charges you ten bucks for a bottle of artisan cider that's not even cloudy.

If Analiese had a flagpole, what flag would she fly? She says she's always preferred New Zealand's to Australia's because New Zealand celebrates its Māori culture. She sets off back down the highway, finds lunch again at Zac's on the way, and will get back to Hobart in time to meet her mother and stepfather at the airport and take them home: they're coming to help with a few jobs on the farm.

In citrus season, Analiese preserves lemons. People give her quinces to do the same, and last year a woman gave her twenty kilos of crabapples. Analiese returned them to her beautifully pickled.

'So many people either have no time or don't know what to do with their produce.'

She has learned a lot since leaving Quay, since throwing chairs at her father, since walking over broken glass in a Michelin kitchen, since being told to leave the first kitchen she ever worked in. Now she says you can't stick around waiting for someone to come and save you. She kept hoping if she moved back to Australia, she and her boyfriend would open a restaurant together and everything would be fine. But then he left for New York and she was alone, and she didn't leave the house for three days.

'You need to think about all the things that make you happy,' Mailing told her, and came round with a whiteboard to help. The sisters made a list of all the times Analiese remembered being really happy, and drew together the common threads: being outdoors and in nature, hiking ...

There are two versions of Analiese, both of which are true, and are probably true of all of us. One version jumps on the bed and drinks champagne from a plastic cup while wearing Miu Miu red velvet shoes and a feather boa. The other is under the duvet, feeling the dark and the cold, with spiders in her hair and sawdust on her clothes after knocking back a bottle of red.

Since realising she had to *stop waiting for fuckin' someone on a white horse to come in and save her because they're not going to*, she feels heaps better. Her decision not to work in fine dining at the moment is part of this shift. It's so intense and kind of shit, although she does still love it, but she also likes what she's doing now. She likes taking it a little slower.

'Maybe it's just about reworking how things are in a fine dining restaurant so they're not going to make me collapse at the end of the day.'

At Franklin she serves food that certain people want and pay well for, and she is happy producing it, served in a restaurant without tablecloths, that somehow manages to take the pressure off the whole show and means she doesn't have to work eighteen-hour days.

'Chill fine dining,' she calls it.

One of her chefs asked her if he should have a five-year plan. The old Analiese would have said, 'Yes, definitely have a plan of where you want to be, and what you want to be doing, and envisage what your restaurant looks like.'

But then five years ago she never imagined she would be living in rural Tasmania. Now she thinks having a plan isn't necessary.

'Just do whatever you're doing and do it well, and just go with the flow and do what makes you happy at the time. When you do that, it also seems to be when you're doing what you're meant to be doing and then people pay attention. As fake as it is, you can kind of tell on social media when someone is being genuine, and people respond to that. I moved here to get away from Sydney and all the bullshit and being constantly hungover and just partying and checking Instagram or Facebook twenty times a day and stuff that was bad for my mental health.'

When she first moved to Tasmania she didn't open her computer for six months. 'I needed to get that out of my life for a while.' And, when she moved into her Huonville farmhouse after two years renting on the D'Entrecasteaux Channel at Woodbridge, she still didn't have the internet on at home.

She moved down to live the quiet life and hike and dive, but the world works in mysterious ways, and now there are probably more people hounding her than ever before. A lot of the things she was trying to get away from seem to have followed her here.

She thinks that maybe, when people see someone doing something that they believe in, they are drawn to it. 'Somehow they can tell you believe in it and want a slice of the action.'

So what do you do when you start encountering what you were getting away from in the place where you're trying to get away from it?

'I haven't quite found the answer ... I guess I'm in the middle of it.'

At night, Analiese gets home, lights a fire, pours a glass of red wine, then lies down on the couch to read.

'This is what I want it to be like. There is no voice inside my head. I just found somewhere I liked and put my things in it.'

In the valley there is a rainbow. She thinks of Tasmania as the land of rainbows. She's never seen so many rainbows in her life.

Shore diving at Fossil Cove, Blackmans Bay

Collecting sea lettuce and dead man's fingers in
rock pools with friend and fellow chef Jo Barrett

Analiese's first experience hunting and cooking
with Cape Barren goose on Flinders Island

Fishing for flathead and making beachside snacks

EPILOGUE

It's not long since Analiese made her momentous decision, rolled the dice and resigned from her job as head chef at Franklin. The upside is that, instead of feeling like she lives on a farmstay, she gets to be home more than half the time to harvest potatoes, make better friends with her goats, plant herbs, deal with all the things she now has time for, and cook the way she likes.

Then the coronavirus pandemic hit. She watched as her friends in restaurants served ever-fewer customers and learned to deal with social distancing. When she flew back to Tasmania from a cooking class in Sydney, she found out she was on the same plane as someone diagnosed with coronavirus and had to self-isolate in Huonville for fourteen days. When stage three lockdown was brought in, Tasmania's border was closed, and Analiese had six months' work cancelled overnight.

Analiese had no choice but to stay home. She saw only Bruce, a friend from nearby Flowerpot who she lived with for a short time when she first moved to Tasmania. Back then, he taught her how to make cheese and charcuterie. This time it was how to kill chickens. She fed herself by foraging and raiding the wild hedgerows: pine mushrooms, windfall apples and blackberries. Because suddenly, she had the time.

She realised how much she loved condiments and making jams that were shelf stable, giving everything she could another life. She had time to refine recipes and start writing them down in a grey notebook she calls her quarantine 2020 cookbook, 'so I can look back on it one day and show this is what I ate, what I did and how I lived'.

Her hallway smells of cider apples. Boxes of them, all foraged, are stacked up against the walls. Far from her smart time in fine dining, it feels old world and wholesome. Her preservation days are just starting. She gets to ring her mum and ask her about what size Fowler's Vacola jar she should use. It's all part of being fearless. Whether she's standing at Kimberley, watching over a huge pot of blackberry jam, or diving on Flinders Island for greenlip abs, she has no sense of holding back.

'I once was a girl who didn't own trousers or flat shoes,' she says. 'Only high heels. And look at me now. Dungarees and Blunnies. My mother is probably the proudest of me she's ever been!'

NEW ZEALAND

Cracking open a sea urchin, cleaning it in the ocean, and eating off a dive knife feels like the way you're meant to eat them

Sea Urchin Farinata

I grew up in coastal New Zealand, the land of the bach, of weekends spent snapper
fishing, collecting pipis in buckets and boiling them with samphire on an outdoor stove.
At that age I hadn't yet learnt to appreciate the sweet, iodine taste of kina (the Māori
name for sea urchin). Now, though, a chickpea farinata (pancake) cooked
in a campfire or woodfired oven with sea urchin and some soured cream is one
of my favourite snacks.

Serves 2

2 whole sea urchins (10 pieces
of sea urchin roe)
100 g (3½ oz) besan (chickpea)
flour
240 ml (8 fl oz) water
½ teaspoon salt
2 tablespoons olive oil
60 g (2 oz) crème fraîche
20 samphire tips
5 dill sprigs

To clean the sea urchin, use a small pair of scissors to pierce
through the opening on top, then cut a roughly 5 cm (2 in)
circle. Shake out the piece of shell and the urchin's innards;
the roe should stay attached inside. Using a teaspoon, lift the
roe pieces out one by one and gently wash in saltwater or a
clean 3% salt brine, then drain.

Whisk the flour and water until smooth, then add the salt. I find
you get a better result if you make the batter the day before and
let it sit overnight. Sometimes, I add dried herbs and spices,
such as green onion top powder, lovage or thyme.

At Franklin we would bake these in a 250°C (480°F) woodfired
oven, but at home, just preheat your oven to the same
temperature.

Pour the oil into a cast-iron, heavy-based 22 cm (8¾ in) pan,
followed by the batter. Cook in the oven for approximately
12 minutes, or until set, golden underneath and lightly
coloured on top.

To serve, smear the crème fraîche over the pancake, top with
cleaned sea urchin, samphire and dill, then some flaky sea salt.
You can also cut the pancake into wedges to make individual
snacks.

This chickpea pancake is great as a carb-based vehicle for
other toppings too, such as broad beans, peas and fresh curd,
tomatoes, cured meat – the list goes on.

The joy of cooking from your childhood: abalone fritters and white bread
eaten at the beach are a reminder of growing up in New Zealand

Abalone Fritters with Bread and Butter (AKA Tip Top Tacos)

These fritters are about as old-school Kiwi as you can get. They come with memories of the shore, attaching an old enamel hand mincer to a picnic table and mincing pāua (the Māori name for abalone) to fry in patties on the barbecue. These days it seems like a very luxurious thing to do, and even though I now have more refined abalone recipes I still make them as a beachside snack for friends when I've been diving.

**Serves 4
(2 fritters each)**

1 abalone (weight in shell 400 g/14 oz, or 170 g/6 oz abalone meat; you can use fresh or frozen, either will work)
½ shallot, finely chopped
1 egg white
¼ bunch coriander (cilantro)
½ teaspoon chilli condiment, such as sambal or sriracha
100 g (3½ oz) soft butter
8 slices soft white sandwich bread*
any other condiments you deem fit

Clean the abalone by removing it from the shell, pulling the guts away from the meat and trimming off any leftover pieces. I often use a small pair of scissors for this.

Dice the abalone into 2 cm (¾ in) pieces and either run twice through a hand mincer or pulse in a food processor until no large chunks remain. Combine with the shallot, egg white, coriander and chilli condiment and season with sea salt to taste. Mix well, then use your hands to shape 8 balls.

Heat a heavy-based frying pan. Add about 20 g (¾ oz) of the butter, then drop an abalone ball into the pan – it should be hot enough that it sizzles – and flatten to form a fritter. Fry each for approximately 2–3 minutes, adding more butter if required, flipping when coloured underneath.

Butter your bread, then add the fritters and any condiments you want, such as lemon, sweet chilli sauce or tartare sauce.

*New Zealand's cheap white bread is called Tip Top, hence this recipe's name. Just grab whatever local brand you have that's reminiscent of sausage sizzles and beachside snacks.

Abalone and XO Butter Egg Noodles

Abalone and XO Butter Egg Noodles

This dish is something I throw together a lot at home for friends and family. It's exceptionally easy, and the feedback you get seems to drastically outweigh the actual time spent in the kitchen. It was inspired by the noodle dishes my mum used to make for us growing up, but I've added things I normally have in my fridge and that she would never have put in.

Serves 4

300–400 g (10½–14 oz) live abalone*
400 g (14 oz) fresh Chinese egg noodles (you can use fresh pasta as a substitute, see opposite)
120 g (4½ oz) butter
3 garlic cloves, minced
2 baby bok choy
80 g (2¾ oz) XO sauce
60 g (2 oz) spring onions (scallions), finely chopped
juice of 1 lemon
crispy fried shallots, to garnish

Preheat a steamer, either stovetop or electric. Place the abalone shell-side down and steam for 50 minutes, or until it can be pierced easily with a skewer. Remove the abalone, take it out of the shell and clean off the guts. Thinly slice it with a sharp knife.

Bring a saucepan of salted water to the boil and blanch the noodles for 30 seconds, then drain, reserving some of the water if you like a slightly wetter sauce.

In a large sauté pan, melt half the butter. Add the garlic and fry it out gently on a low heat, making sure it doesn't colour, about 3 minutes. Add the sliced abalone, fry it in the butter for 1–2 minutes, then add the bok choy, XO sauce and the rest of the butter. Stir as the bok choy wilts and the sauce emulsifies, 1–2 minutes. Add the spring onions and still-warm noodles and toss everything together.

Season with lemon juice and test to see if it requires salt. Add a little of the noodle-blanching water to thin out the sauce, if desired. Top with crispy fried shallots for texture. Often, I eat this with a chilli and Sichuan pepper sauce, such as Lao Gan Ma, as a condiment.

*You can reserve and dehydrate the abalone liver and stomach, then grind them to a powder to make an 'abalone salt' for seasoning fish and vegetables (see also recipe on page 153). This is a technique we used a lot at Franklin.

Mussel Butter Tagliatelle

Imagine a roasted mussel butter, redolent of wild fennel and seaweed, tossed through a super yolky, silky pasta, with fresh mussels and fried breadcrumbs. It took me a while to discover my love for mussels after being scarred in my youth by large, overcooked, rubbery bivalves. Now that I have, all I want is to pickle, steam, roast, grill them, make sauces with them and toss them through pasta.

Serves 4

1 quantity Pasta (see below)
100 g (3½ oz) mussel meat (around 500 g/1 lb 2 oz in their shells), plus 20 extra mussels for serving
35 g (1¼ oz) Wakame jam (page 230)
juice of 2 lemons
2 g (¹⁄₁₀ oz) yuzu kosho (a Japanese condiment made from fermented yuzu peel, chillies and salt), or any fermented chilli paste
200 g (7 oz) butter, cut into cubes
50 g (1¾ oz) panko breadcrumbs
2 tablespoons olive oil
wild fennel fronds, to garnish, or dill if unavailable
chervil, to garnish

Pasta

240 g (8½ oz) egg yolks (approximately 15)
1 egg
2 teaspoons olive oil
500 g (1 lb 2 oz) 00 flour
fine semolina, for rolling

To make the pasta dough, lightly whisk the egg yolks, whole egg and olive oil in a bowl. In a food processor or stand mixer fitted with the paddle attachment, combine the flour and egg mixture and mix on the lowest speed until it resembles large crumbs. This is a very dry dough, so it may feel like it will never come together, but it will. Knead for an extra 2 minutes after the dough comes together, then continue to knead lightly by hand. Shape the dough into a flat brick, cover tightly and rest overnight in the fridge.

Roll out the pasta. Because this is a very yolk-heavy dough, it has a high amount of fat, making it harder to roll when cold. Remove it from the fridge and bring to room temperature before rolling it out and cutting to tagliatelle thickness.

If you have a steamer, steam all the mussels with a tray underneath to catch the juices. Alternatively, bring 250 ml (8½ fl oz/1 cup) water to the boil in a wide-based saucepan, then throw your mussels in, stir them around, put the lid on and steam until they just open, 2–3 minutes. Deshell and debeard them. Reserve the mussel juice.

Set aside 20 mussels for serving. In a blender, combine the rest of the mussels, 100 ml (3½ fl oz) of the reserved hot mussel juice, wakame jam, lemon juice and yuzu kosho and blend until smooth. Add the butter slowly, a little at a time, until the sauce is fully emulsified. Check the seasoning, then pass it through a fine chinois (conical sieve/strainer) or sieve.

Toss the breadcrumbs and oil in a frying pan and cook out over a medium heat, stirring constantly, until golden all over, approximately 5 minutes. Season with flaky sea salt.

Bring a large pot of salted water to the boil. Drop in the pasta, cooking for approximately 2 minutes. Check for doneness by biting into one of the strands: it should be fairly firm. Drain.

In a large pan, warm the sauce. Toss through the hot pasta and remaining mussels, then divide between plates. Garnish with the fresh herbs and breadcrumbs.

Chargrilled Oyster Mushrooms with Wakame Sabayon

Just a supremely delicious way to eat mushrooms. When I had this on as a snack at Franklin, guests would rave about it. Now I whip it out for events and dinner parties when I want to impress.

Makes 8 skewers

300 g (10½ oz) oyster mushrooms
20 g (¾ oz) clarified butter*
1 tablespoon Wakame jam (page 230), to serve

Sabayon
140 g (5 oz) clarified butter
3 egg yolks
2 teaspoons water
2 teaspoons mushroom soy sauce**

Trim the thick bases of the oyster mushrooms and separate them from each other. Thread 25 g (1 oz) of mushrooms onto a skewer, then repeat with the rest.

To make the sabayon, melt 140 g (5 oz) clarified butter in a small saucepan. Fill another small saucepan one-quarter with water and bring to a simmer. In a heat-conducting bowl, such as stainless steel, whisk the yolks, water and mushroom soy. Place the bowl over the simmering water and whisk until a sabayon (a custardy sauce) is reached: it should be thick and smooth, and hold a trail on its surface when the whisk is dragged across it.

Take the bowl off the heat and slowly pour in the butter, whisking continuously to emulsify. Check the seasoning and add sea salt if necessary.

There are several ways you can cook the mushroom skewers. I have pan-fried them in clarified butter, but my favourite way is to brush them with butter, season with salt and grill them over charcoal. They cook very quickly, in approximately 1½–2 minutes. Turn once to get an even colour on both sides.

Remove from the grill and serve with the sabayon and wakame jam.

* Clarified butter is butter with the milk solids removed. To clarify butter, melt the butter over a low heat. Let is simmer and skim off the foam that rises to the top. Next, line a sieve with muslin (cheesecloth) and strain the butter through the sieve into a container or jar. The butter amount reduces by around one-third in the clarifying process. It will keep in the refrigerator for several months.

**Mushroom soy is made with dried shiitake mushrooms. It can be substituted with regular soy sauce.

Chinese Breakfast Eggs and Brown Rice

I think this is my all-time favourite breakfast, so simple it almost seems strange to include it here. My mum used to cook eggs this way for my sister and me when we were young. I've switched between western and eastern breakfasts all my life, having been brought up on a diet of rice and congee. But then I spent three weeks in Japan once, where I started every day with rice, fish and eggs. After that I stopped craving bread and dairy in the morning and realised that I enjoy the feeling of wellbeing these ingredients give me.

Serves 2

200 g (7 oz) brown
    biodynamic rice
4 eggs
1½ tablespoons soy
1½ tablespoons neutral oil
8 Fermented shiitake
    mushrooms, cut into quarters
    (page 220)
drizzle of untoasted sesame oil
shichimi togarashi, to garnish

Wash the brown rice and drain it thoroughly. Place it in either a rice cooker or a suitably sized saucepan with a lid with 500 ml (17 oz/2 cups) water and cook until the water is absorbed and the rice is tender, about 40 minutes. Once the rice is cooked, I let it sit off the heat for about 5 minutes.

In a small bowl, whisk the eggs and soy. Heat the oil in a non-stick or seasoned 25 cm (10 in) frying pan. When the oil is hot, but before it starts to smoke, pour in the egg mix. Stir with a spatula, bringing the eggs on the outside of the pan to the centre, lifting the egg off the bottom as you go. The eggs should be set around the sides and underneath, but still retain some moisture on top. They will cook fast, approximately 1–2 minutes.

Slide the eggs straight onto bowls of rice, add the mushrooms, drizzle with sesame oil and give them a shake of togarashi. I like to add whatever vegetables or pickles I have around – kimchi, mushrooms, greens, broccoli or tamari-toasted seeds and nuts.

Oca with Spelt, Miso and Roasted Pears

For a long time, I wanted to make a dish out of oca (or yam, as it's more commonly known), but it eluded me. Then one day I picked some up at the market, roasted them with baby pears I had hanging around, deglazed the lot with butter and honey vinegar, and added some organic spelt bound with miso. It's definitely a vegetarian good time.

Serves 4

240 g (8½ oz) organic spelt grain
500 ml (17 fl oz/2 cups) cold water
4 thyme sprigs
1½ tablespoons grapeseed oil
400 g (14 oz) oca, scrubbed to remove any dirt
1 ripe pear, cored and cut into eighths
2 tablespoons Honey vinegar (page 227)
140 g (5 oz) butter
40 g (1½ oz) spelt miso
10 sorrel leaves, shredded, to garnish

Preheat the oven to 165°C (330°F).

Combine the spelt grain, cold water, thyme and salt in a saucepan and cook out slowly on a low to medium heat. It should take approximately 45 minutes. Drain and remove the thyme.

While the spelt is cooking, heat a heavy-based, ovenproof pan. Add the oil and oca and season with some sea salt. Cook in the oven for approximately 30 minutes, tossing every 10 minutes, until caramelised on the outside and soft at the centre. Add the pear and continue to cook for another 10 minutes.

Pull the pan out of the oven and put it on a low heat. Add the honey vinegar and 30 g (1 oz) butter and swirl to glaze the oca and pear.

In a saucepan, heat the spelt, remaining butter and miso until the spelt is hot and the liquid has reduced to form an emulsified sauce, about 5 minutes. Season if required. Top with the oca and pear, then garnish with sorrel.

White Elf Mushroom with Soy-cured Egg Yolk and Slippery Jack

White Elf Mushroom with Soy-cured Egg Yolk and Slippery Jack

It's extremely exciting when I receive a message from Will at Forest Fungi telling me 'the elves are back'. He's referring to a large, white species of oyster mushroom with a flavour and texture similar to abalone that likes to grow when it's snowing outside. It has become my favourite mushroom to cook and serve to guests – truly a beautiful piece of produce.

Serves 2

250 g (9 oz) white elf
  mushroom, or substitute with
  shiitake or lion's mane
130 g (4½ oz) butter
2 garlic cloves
4 thyme sprigs
2 tablespoons mushroom soy
  sauce (see Note on page 117)
3 teaspoons brown rice mirin
1 egg yolk
5 g (¼ oz) slippery jack powder
  (dried, powdered slippery jack
  mushrooms), or substitute
  with mushroom powder

Trim the stalk of the mushroom if necessary. In a sauté pan, melt the butter over a medium heat, then add the garlic and thyme. Season the mushroom with salt and pepper and add it to the hot pan. You want it to colour gently and cook through without taking the butter too far. I turn it after 3 minutes, then cook for another 2 minutes. Remove from the pan and let it drain and rest on absorbent towel.

In a small bowl, combine the soy and mirin, then add the egg yolk and let it cure for 2 minutes.

Slice the mushroom thinly and spread it in a serving bowl. Drain the egg yolk, making sure to reserve the curing liquid, and nestle it in with the mushrooms. Spoon a tablespoon of curing liquid over the top and sprinkle the whole thing with slippery jack powder.

Brown Sugar-cured Hot Smoked Trout

Once a year growing up, my family would decamp to Lake Taupo for trout season. This involved some atrociously bad fly fishing, sitting in rocky thermal heated streams and eventually taking a charter on the lake to actually catch some fish. As a fourteen-year-old interested in cooking, I smoked out many hotel rooms and set off countless fire alarms trying to smoke fish for my family. This is the method I use now, at work and at home. Once you get a feel for cooking the fish, it becomes a truly enjoyable thing to make.

Serves 2

100 g (3½ oz) fine sea salt
100 g (3½ oz) brown sugar
1 × 500 g (1 lb 2 oz) whole
   rainbow or brown trout,
   gutted and scaled

In a bowl, mix the salt and sugar thoroughly. Sprinkle some into a tray. Put the clean fish down on top, then open the cavity and evenly sprinkle the inside with the curing mix. Pat the rest on top, then cover and refrigerate the fish for 12 hours or overnight.

Wash the cure off the fish, pat dry and leave on a tray in the fridge so the skin can dry, approximately 6 hours.

Preheat a smoker to 60°C (140°F) and use your choice of wood chips. In New Zealand, we would often use manuka, a native variety of tea tree. Once the chips are smoking and the chamber is preheated, lay the fish on an oiled rack (this will be important for removing it after). I cook it to an internal temperature of 58°C (136°F) so it is still extremely moist and the protein is just set, but you can take it higher if that is your preference.

I have also done this many times in an oven. Just preheat to 58°C (136°F), get a small tray of wood chips smoking and slide it into the bottom of the oven while your fish is in there.

Looking for crayfish off Killiecrankie with local
legend Mick Grimshaw

Crayfish Cocktail | Crayfish and Lovage Omelette

Crayfish Cocktail

This is a dish that came to be when I got home to Tasmania from Sydney one day and found a friend sitting on my lawn, holding a crayfish, with the intention of staying for dinner. All I had in the house were potatoes, lovage growing in the garden and eggs from the chickens. Thus the crayfish potato salad was born.

Serves 2–4

1 × 500 g (1 lb 2 oz) live crayfish
350 g (12½ oz) pink eye
  potatoes, or other new waxy
  potatoes
1 quantity Mayonnaise (see
  opposite)
50 g (1¾ oz) sour cream
1 shallot, finely diced
10 lovage leaves, chiffonnaded
  (finely shredded into ribbons)
2 baby gem lettuce
1 lemon

Put your crayfish either in the freezer or an ice bath of water to chill it down. Bring a large pot of water to the boil and fully submerge the crayfish in it. Cook for 7 minutes, making sure it doesn't come back to a rolling boil. Remove the crayfish, drain and leave to sit on a tray at room temperature for 30 minutes.

Scrub the potatoes and place in a saucepan of cold salted water on the stove. Bring to a simmer, turn down the heat and cook until tender but not falling apart. Take off the heat and leave to cool in the water. Then drain completely and dice each potato in roughly 2 cm (¾ in) cubes. When at room temperature, mix with the mayonnaise, sour cream, shallot and lovage.

To prepare the tail, taking the head of the crayfish in one hand and the tail in the other, twist the tail away from the head. Then, you can either crack the tail gently with your hands and peel away the shell or, using scissors, cut either side of the soft carapace underneath, then remove this piece and the tail from the shell. Once this is achieved, using a sharp knife, cut the tail down the centre lengthways and remove the vein running the length of the tail. Slice the tail into 1 cm (½ in) medallions and reserve.

To serve, trim the base of the lettuce leaves and arrange a bed of them on a platter, top with the medallions of crayfish, a squeeze of lemon, cracked black pepper and the dressed potato.

Crayfish and Lovage Omelette

When you wake up and realise you have a crayfish head and some lovage and mayonnaise, plus eggs from your chickens, what do you make? A crayfish omelette of course! It's a great way to use all the fiddly bits out of the head and leg. I always make a friend pick the crayfish while I fluff around collecting eggs.

Makes 1 omelette

crayfish head and legs left
    over from a previous recipe
    (see opposite)
10 lovage leaves, chiffonnaded
    (finely shredded into ribbons)
3 eggs
½ tablespoon grapeseed oil
5 dill sprigs

Mayonnaise
1 garlic clove, minced
2 egg yolks
1 tablespoon lemon juice
1 tablespoon white-wine vinegar
1 tablespoon dijon mustard
125 ml (4 fl oz/½ cup) olive oil
125 ml (4 fl oz/½ cup)
    grapeseed oil

To make the mayonnaise, combine the garlic, egg yolks, lemon juice, vinegar and mustard in a blender and blend until smooth. Combine the oils and, with the blender still running, slowly drizzle them in, making sure they're emulsifying. Season with sea salt to taste.

Snap the legs off the crayfish, then pick the meat out of them and the head. Roughly dice the meat, then add just enough mayonnaise to bind it together. Mix through the lovage. Check the seasoning: it should taste like your dream crayfish sandwich filling. Store the leftover mayonnaise in the fridge and use it in other dishes. It will keep for several weeks.

In a bowl, lightly whisk the eggs and season with sea salt. Gently preheat a seasoned omelette or non-stick frying pan on a fairly low heat. Add the oil, followed by the egg mixture. Using a spatula or fork, agitate the eggs with one hand, holding the pan in the other, lifting the egg off the base and sides and stirring it back to the middle. Flatten the eggs with your spatula and let them set gently. When the omelette is still baveuse (slightly runny) on top, fold one side over toward the middle, then the other, and invert onto a plate. Top with the crayfish mayonnaise mix and dill and season with pepper and flaky sea salt.

Possum Sausages

On the farm in the Waikato it was normal to hear farmers shooting possum at night. I grew up knowing they were an introduced species with an out-of-control population. I wish I had known then, as I know now, that they are also a great traditional source of meat. Once I got over the mental stigma of eating possum, I began to explore different ways to cook with it. This is a recipe for possum sausages developed by one of my close friends in Tasmania, Bruce Kemp. Together we've spent many hours breaking down possums and wallabies to make sausages and salami, pushing our own preconceptions of what constitutes food.

Makes 3 kg (6 lb 10 oz) of sausages

2 kg (4 lb 6 oz) possum meat
450 g (1 lb) pork back fat
2 teaspoons caster (superfine) sugar
3 tablespoons paprika (either Spanish or sweet Hungarian)
1½ tablespoons sumac
1 tablespoon chilli flakes
1 tablespoon cracked black pepper
1 tablespoon ground cumin
1 teaspoon ground aniseed
20 g (¾ oz) roasted garlic, minced
125 ml (4 fl oz/½ cup) chilled red wine
60 ml (2 fl oz/¼ cup) ice water
225 g (8 oz) roasted red capsicum (bell pepper)
1.8 m (6 ft) sheep sausage casing

Cut the meat and pork fat into 10 cm (4 in) cubes. Partially freeze before grinding: it shouldn't be fully frozen, but very cold and quite firm.

Using the medium disc on your grinder, grind the meat and fat. Using either your hands or a stand mixer fitted with the paddle attachment, mix the meat with the sugar, spices, garlic, wine and water for 2 minutes.

Put the mix into a sausage stuffer, thread on the casing, tie one end off and fill. Twist the sausages to the desired length, then hang and refrigerate overnight. These can now be smoked, fried, poached or barbecued until the internal temperature is 70°C (160°F).

Manuka Honey Madeleines

I've been experimenting with taking processed sugar out of some of my recipes and replacing it with more natural alternatives, such as honey and malt syrups. This is one of the recipes that adapted exceptionally well to honey, and I love the flavour the madeleines get from intense ones such as manuka and leatherwood. For me, these cakes are best served straight from the oven. They don't benefit from being kept for too long!

Makes 24 madeleines

170 g (6 oz) butter, plus some
   for brushing the metal mould
3 eggs
185 g (6½ oz) manuka or
   leatherwood honey, or other
   honey as preferred
160 g (5½ oz) plain flour
¼ teaspoon salt
¼ teaspoon baking powder
soured cream, to serve

Apricot Jam
250 g (9 oz) apricots
2½ tablespoons water
50 g (1¾ oz) honey

Preheat the oven to 180°C (350°F). Melt the butter and let cool to room temperature.

In a stand mixer, whisk the eggs and honey until light and fluffy, approximately 10 minutes. In a separate bowl, sift the dry ingredients, then add them to the egg mix and fold by hand. Once the dry ingredients are incorporated, gently fold in the cooled melted butter. Chill in the fridge for approximately 30 minutes.

To make the jam, take the seeds out of the apricots, then roughly dice them. Combine with the water and honey in a saucepan and cook on a medium heat for approximately 10 minutes, or until a jammy consistency is reached.

Butter a madeleine mould with a pastry brush. I use a 12-cake non-stick metal one; the old copper madeleine moulds are amazing, but I would grease and flour them first. Fill each indentation half full and bake for 10 minutes. They should be set and golden, with minimal colour on top and light brown underneath.

Serve immediately with soured cream and jam.

TRAVELS

Choosing vegetables from grower James Hutchinson
at Longley Organic Farm

Cashew Miso Cream with Young Vegetables

I suppose every chef that ever worked for Michel Bras has their version or homage to his famous dish The Gargouillou, comprised of over fifty different vegetables, herbs and flowers, purées, pickles, fruits and French country ham. This one incredible dish taught me so much about seasonality, flavour, ingredient combinations, and how truly great dishes transcend food trends and fads. This is a very simple salad, loosely inspired by my time at Bras, that basically includes every vegetable we have in the fridge in early summer in Tasmania. An autumn, spring or winter version would be just as great – just different.

Serves 4

½ baby romanesco
1 baby cucumber
1 baby gem lettuce
4 yellow butter beans
2 Paris market carrots
2 zucchini (courgette) flowers
2 purple carrots
2 hakurei turnips
1 baby Chioggia (candy stripe)
    beetroot (beet) and its leaves
1 pink turnip
6 amaranth leaves
6 blueberries
4 purple basil leaves
4 shiso leaves
4 Greek basil tips
olive oil, to serve

Cashew Miso Cream
250 g (9 oz) raw cashew nuts
220 ml (7½ fl oz) water
50 g (1¾ oz) Chickpea miso
    (page 220) or a sweet, nutty
    brown rice miso
¼ teaspoon salt

Soak the cashews in cold water for at least 2 hours or overnight. Drain, then combine with the water, miso and salt and blend on high speed until smooth. It may take a while. Clean and slice the vegetables, keeping edible leaves on where possible. All vegetables in this particular salad are raw, sliced thinly or into florets or left whole depending on the vegetable. It's about taking a whole bunch of beautiful, in-season vegetables and treating them like crudités, dragging them through the cashew dip.

Dress a plate with the cashew miso cream and arrange the vegetables on top. Dress with olive oil and salt and pepper to taste.

Green Garlic Oil Flatbread

I'm not sure where my flatbread addiction started, but I can remember obsessively buying it daily in the Fès medina to eat with yoghurt and honey. I drove across Morocco to learn to make flatbread at the feet of an old Moroccan lady in Moulay Idriss, in a whitewashed house full of turtles, rabbits and ducks, where the only language spoken was Arabic. We communicated with hand gestures and cooked cross-legged on the floor. This particular recipe started as a friend's pizza dough recipe from Japan, but it works equally well for flatbread. I made and sold many at Franklin, but I've also made it at the beach to serve with sea urchin straight from the ocean, served it with a whole-grilled wallaby cooked over coals at a friend's barbecue, and taken it away on a boat to make pizzas in the middle of the ocean. Suffice to say it's never let me down and I have a whole host of friends who tell me it's become an indispensable part of their kitchen repertoire.

Makes 6 pieces of flatbread

300 g (10½ oz) strong flour
(or any flour with a high
gluten content)
100 g (3½ oz) kamut flour*
100 g (3½ oz) whole wheat flour
15 g (½ oz) sea salt
3.5 g (⅛ oz) dry yeast
400 ml (13½ fl oz) water
neutral oil, for cooking

Green Garlic Oil
3 green garlic stalks
100 ml (3½ fl oz) grapeseed oil
100 ml (3½ fl oz) olive oil

Combine the dry ingredients in a bowl, then pour in the water. Mix by hand until the dough comes together, then continue mixing until it's smooth, but still sticky.

Put the ball of dough in an oiled bowl and cover. I'm pretty lazy with home breadmaking, so I give it a fold and put it in the fridge overnight to prove. The next day, let it come to room temperature, turn it out onto a lightly floured surface, knock it back to take some of the air out and portion it into balls. I weigh out 60 g (2 oz) pieces or go by the size of flatbread I'm after.

Arrange the balls onto a lightly floured baking tray and leave to prove again.

To make the green garlic oil, thinly slice the garlic. Heat 2 tablespoons of grapeseed oil in a heavy-based pan and sauté the garlic gently until soft, but not coloured. Combine all ingredients in a blender and blend until smooth. Season with sea salt to taste.

To cook the flatbreads, I simply heat a frying pan with some neutral oil over a medium heat, grab a ball of dough and stretch (or roll) it out, then drop it in the pan and fry for 2 minutes on each side until golden and crispy.

To serve, brush the cooked flatbreads with the green garlic oil.

*Kamut flour is made from khorasan wheat and is available from wholefood shops and some supermarkets.

Roasted Celtuce with Egg Butter and Abalone Salt

Celtuce is a stem lettuce very popular in China and Taiwan. I first came across it when working in France, where it often gets steamed and then roasted in foaming butter until soft and nutty. When picked at the right time, before it gets bitter, it is truly one of the most delicious vegetables. If you don't happen to have it, you can sub it in this recipe for asparagus, broccoli or any other vegetable that goes well with a hint of seafood and some buttery, eggy goodness.

Serves 2

2 whole stalks celtuce
15 g (½ oz) butter, for cooking the celtuce
dried abalone guts, ground to a powder

Egg Butter
2 eggs
15 g (½ oz) cultured butter, softened
15 g (½ oz) brown butter
½ teaspoon light soy sauce
⅛ bunch chives
⅛ bunch chervil
⅛ bunch parsley
⅛ bunch tarragon
juice of 1 lemon

Take the outer leaves off the celtuce, keeping any that are in good condition. Peel down the outside of the stem until the bright green inside is exposed and there are no fibrous strands left. Blanch or steam the stems until they are still slightly firm in the centre, approximately 5 minutes. Refresh in an ice bath, then drain.

For the egg butter, boil the eggs for 8 minutes, then refresh in an ice bath. Peel the eggs and, using a fork, break them apart and mix with the soft butter, brown butter, soy, herbs and some freshly ground pepper to taste. Season with lemon juice.

In a frying pan on a medium heat, melt the butter. When it starts to foam, add the celtuce and cook on all sides, browning gently for about 4 minutes. Pour the egg butter into a bowl, top with the celtuce and season with the abalone salt. Garnish with the young celtuce leaves.

Confit Lamb Ribs with Date Syrup and Toasted Spices

Confit Lamb Ribs with Date Syrup and Toasted Spices

I came across some crisp-fried lamb ribs in Chinatown in Queens once when I was eating my way through New York City. The dish was served as a whole piece of fatty ribs and belly, crispy on the outside and absolutely smothered by a pile of toasted sesame and cumin seeds that I thought would be overpowering, but which actually cut through the meat perfectly. Later, when I was in Morocco, where spices, date syrup and lamb were some of the readily available ingredients in the medina where I would shop every day, I created this version.

Serves 4

1.5 kg (3 lb 5 oz) lamb ribs
50 g (1¾ oz) salt
olive oil, as needed for cooking the ribs, plus 2 tablespoons for the breadcrumbs
15 g (½ oz) fennel seeds
15 g (½ oz) cumin seeds
120 g (4½ oz) panko breadcrumbs
100 ml (3½ fl oz) date syrup

Sprinkle the lamb ribs all over with the salt. Arrange them on a tray and refrigerate for 8 hours or overnight.

Preheat the oven to 120°C (250°F).

Wash the ribs, pat dry and put in an ovenproof pot, drenching them in olive oil. Bring the heat up slowly on the stove until the olive oil starts to bubble. Transfer to the oven and cook, covered, for approximately 2 hours, or until the ribs are tender and the meat comes easily away from the bone. Take the ribs out of the oil and chill down in the fridge until firm.

Combine the spices in a frying pan over a low heat and toast until fragrant, then pour into a bowl to cool down. Put the panko crumbs and 2 tablespoons oil in the pan and cook, stirring constantly, until crispy and golden. Add the crumbs to the spices, mix together and season with sea salt.

Preheat a deep fryer or stovetop pot of oil to 180°C (350°F). You'll need enough oil to cover the ribs. Take the ribs and cut down between the bones to make individual ribs. Deep fry until brown and crispy on the outside, approximately 5 minutes. Drain and toss them in a bowl with the date syrup. To serve, arrange on a plate and cover with the spiced crumbs.

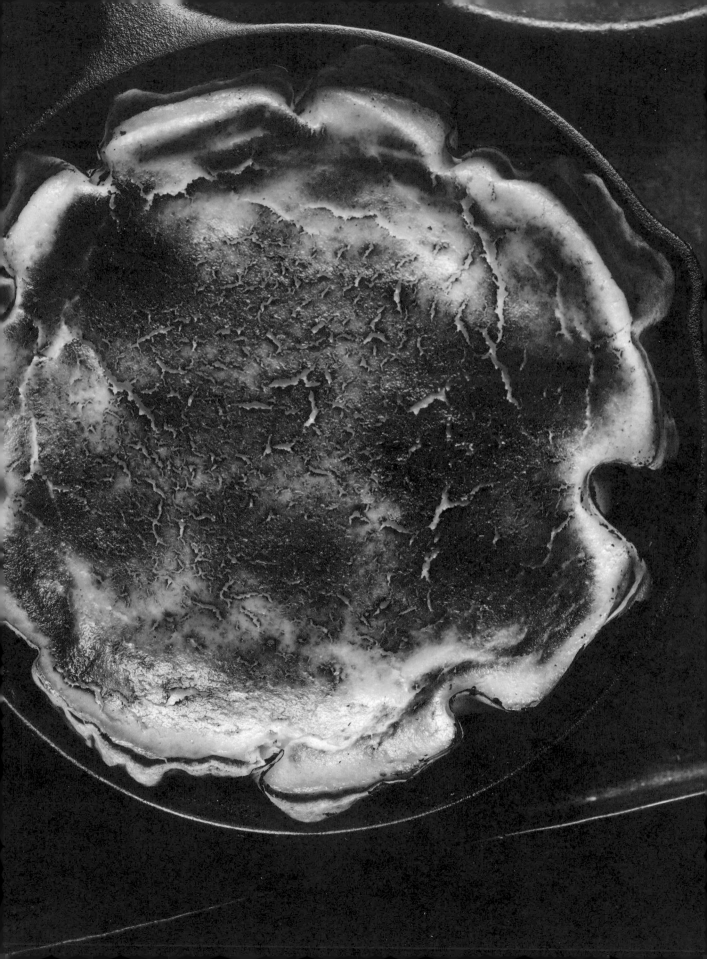

Basque Cheesecake

Basque Cheesecake

When I was living in Basque country, just outside San Sebastian, I became obsessed with several Spanish sweets. Torrija and Basque cheesecake, especially. There is a pintxos bar in the old town of San Sebastian called La Vina, where they specialise in one thing: tarta de queso, or cheesecake. This is literally the only thing I would go there to eat. They bake approximately ten to fourteen cheesecakes a day, all dark topped and paper ruffled, and they always sell out. This is my version. It works well with acidic fruits such as apricots and citrus. I've also made it with poached quince and topped with wild fennel seeds, which was a huge hit. You can either make one large cake (pictured on page 158) or several small ones. If you are going for individual cakes, reduce the baking time to 15 minutes.

Serves 6–8

500 g (1 lb 2 oz) cream cheese, room temperature
160 g (5½ oz) caster (superfine) sugar
¼ teaspoon sea salt
2 eggs
1 egg yolk
260 ml (9 fl oz) cream
10 g (¼ oz) plain (all-purpose) flour
very thinly sliced Meyer lemon, for garnish (optional)

Lemon Purée
2 Meyer lemons
60 g (2 oz) honey
1 tablespoon water

Heat the oven to 180°C (350°F). Grease and line a 25 cm (10 in) pan or cake tin with baking paper, making sure it extends right up the sides, or line individual small cake tins or pans instead.

To make the lemon purée, pierce the lemons all over with a skewer, then immerse in a small saucepan of water. Bring to the boil and cook for 5 minutes. Discard the water and repeat this process two more times; by this stage, the lemons should be soft to the touch.

Drain and blend the lemons with the honey and water until smooth. Pass through a fine chinois (conical sieve/strainer) to get rid of any seed remnants.

In the bowl of a stand mixer using the paddle attachment (or by hand if you feel up to it), beat the cream cheese, sugar and salt until smooth. Add the eggs and beat until smooth. Add the cream and mix thoroughly, but gently so as not to overwork or whip it. Sift the flour over the batter and fold through.

Smooth 100 g (3½ oz) of purée over the base of the pan(s), covering it completely (store whatever's left over in the fridge; it will keep for weeks). Pour in the batter, then put the cake in the oven and bake for approximately 40 minutes, or until golden brown on top but still jiggly in the centre. Let cool at room temperature. Garnish with slices of lemon, if desired.

Pickled Mussels and Octopus with XO Aioli

This is another throwback to my time spent roaming the bars of San Sebastian's old town, becoming more and more enamoured with the food, cider, pace of life and, in particular, the pearly white skewers of octopus drenched in vinegar and oil and served with diced onion and peppers. I suppose this is my take on those pickled octopus pintxos.

Serves 4

20 blue mussels, live in shell
150 ml (5 fl oz) water
100 ml (3½ fl oz) white vinegar
50 g (1¾ oz) sugar
2 white Tokyo turnips (a small, white radish-sized turnip)
150 g (5½ oz) small, tumbled-clean octopus
¼ bunch chives, finely chopped
¼ bunch dill, finely chopped
2 tablespoons olive oil

XO Aioli

2 egg yolks
1 tablespoon white-wine vinegar
1 tablespoon lemon juice
1 tablespoon dijon mustard
1 garlic clove
130 ml (4½ fl oz) grapeseed oil
130 ml (4½ fl oz) olive oil
40 g (1½ oz) XO sauce

Wash the mussels, then steam in a covered metal or bamboo steamer over a pot of boiling water until just opened. Put them in a bowl to collect the juices. Deshell and debeard and put them back into the mussel juice.

In a medium saucepan, combine the water, vinegar and sugar and simmer over a low heat until the sugar is dissolved. Set aside until warm, but not hot. Pour this pickling liquid over the mussels and refrigerate. (Eat the mussels on the day of pickling, if you can. They do keep, but the pickle will continue to firm up the texture over time.)

Cut the turnips into quarters or eighths, depending on size. Pan-fry or grill the octopus over a medium heat until just cooked, approximately 3 minutes, then slice thinly. In a bowl, combine the octopus, mussels, herbs, turnips and olive oil and mix together.

To make the aioli, put the egg yolks, vinegar, lemon juice and mustard in a blender, then microplane in the garlic. Blend until smooth. With the blender running on low, pour in the two oils in a very thin stream, allowing the aioli to emulsify. At the end, fold through the XO sauce and check for seasoning. I often use a stick blender to make it quickly at home.

Spoon some aioli into the base of a large bowl. Top with the pickled seafood and herbs.

I like to serve this with Green garlic oil flatbread (page 152).

Analiese's first year growing potatoes, and realising what a
difference in taste and texture a freshly dug potato makes

Potato Galette

This is one of my all-time favourite potato dishes, based on the Pommes Sarladaises we would make when I worked at The Ledbury in London. It was a once-a-week lunch special, cooked entirely on the stove. Every Sunday I would make five huge pans and spend the next hour constantly rotating them and freaking out about whether they would turn out nicely or be overcoloured. We made a woodfired version when I worked at Franklin, and people would often tell me it was the highlight of their meal.

Serves 4

125 g (4½ oz) clarified butter (see Note on page 117)
900 g (2 lb) or 7 medium waxy potatoes
10 g (¼ oz) flaky sea salt

Preheat the oven to 160°C (320°F). Line a 22 cm (8¾ in) pan with baking paper.

In a small saucepan, melt the butter. Scrub the potatoes and slice them thinly, with a mandoline if you have one, about 2 mm (⅛ in) thick. Toss them in a bowl with the clarified butter and salt until completely coated.

Starting in the centre of the pan, lay the potato in concentric circles, each new slice overlapping the previous one by about two thirds. This is your presentation layer, so you want to make it as tidy as possible! Continue to layer the overlapping potatoes until the pan is full and you've used all the potato. Place another square of baking paper on top, followed by a small round tray, ovenproof plate or even the lid of a pot to provide a bit of weight for pressing down the galette. Cook in the oven for 1 hour, or until a skewer inserted in the centre meets no resistance.

Once cooked, colour up the base on the stove or under the grill (broiler). For the stove method, place the pan on the stove over a low heat, checking the colour periodically. For the grill method, turn out the galette, invert it back into the pan, drizzle with olive oil and place under the grill until coloured. Serve immediately. If serving the next day, once cooked, skip the colouring step, place a small weight on top and press the galette in the fridge overnight. The next day, turn it out, cut into portions and colour the top in a high-heat oven or in a pan.

Potato galette is great as a side dish with any main course or as a vegetarian dish on its own. Some condiments I've served it with:

Garlic yoghurt
Goat's curd (page 230)
Crème fraîche
Pickled walnut mayonnaise
Whipped cod roe
Salsa verde
Chutney or gravy

Potato Gnocchi with Lap Cheong and Kombu Butter

Once upon a time in London, I worked on a gnocchi station in a French restaurant. I would make four to five different kinds of gnocchi every day, some cooked to order, some blanched before service and pan fried. To this day, I have a deep, abiding love for these little potato dumplings, and I like to pair them with flavours and ingredients from other cultures and influences. This is a dish I had on the menu when I was part of a Sydney wine bar and trying to blend my Chinese heritage with the European classics I had been taught. It may sound like an odd combination, but it works. Trust me.

Serves 4

3 lap cheong sausages (dried Chinese pork sausage), thinly sliced
1 bunch kai lan (Chinese broccoli), washed and cut into 5 cm (2 in) lengths
1 tablespoon lemon juice

Gnocchi

1 kg (2 lb 3 oz) floury potatoes
50 g (1¾ oz) finely grated parmesan
2 egg yolks
110 g (4 oz) 00 flour
olive oil, for tossing

Chilli Dressing

50 g (1¾ oz) Lao Gan Ma (crispy chilli and Szechuan pepper sauce), or other chilli sauce
55 ml (1¾ fl oz) olive oil
30 g (1 oz) honey
1 tablespoon black vinegar

Kombu Butter

1 tablespoon shio kombu
100 g (3½ oz) cultured butter, softened
1 teaspoon shiro shoyu (a wheat soy sauce)
1 teaspoon wakame powder

Preheat the oven to 175°C (340°F) and line two baking trays with baking paper and sprinkle with flour.

Wash the potatoes and, with the tip of a knife, score a circle in the skin without cutting much flesh, about 5 mm (¼ in) deep. This will make it easier to break them apart once cooked. Bake directly on a rack for approximately 1 hour, or until soft in the centre. Break the potatoes in half and press the flesh through a drum sieve or put through a ricer.

Weigh out 500 g (1 lb 2 oz) of potato flesh into a bowl. Add the parmesan, egg yolks and a pinch of salt and mix with a spoon. Add the flour and fold in gently, being careful not to overmix. Turn the dough out onto a floured bench. Divide into fourths, then roll each into a thin log. Cut into 2 cm (¾ in) pieces, then place the gnocchi carefully on the prepared trays.

Cook the gnocchi in batches in some lightly simmering salted water. Wait until they float, then give them another 20 seconds before lifting out and putting them in an ice bath. Once all are cooked, drain and lightly toss with olive oil. Refrigerate.

To make the chilli dressing, mix all of the ingredients together.

To make the kombu butter, rehydrate the shio kombu in 2 tablespoons water, then chop and combine with the butter, shoyu and wakame powder.

Heat a large non-stick frying pan over a medium heat and pan-fry the gnocchi in two batches, tossing halfway through to brown both sides. Pan-fry the lap cheong until it starts to render. Return all gnocchi to the pan, add the kai lan and kombu butter, and toss until the leaves start to wilt, approximately 1 minute. Season with lemon juice and salt if needed. Transfer to plates and dress with the chilli dressing.

TASMANIA

Red Cabbage Schnitzel with Anchovy and Bitter Leaves

In Hobart, I've always bought cabbages from an organic farmer named Tony Scherer. He knows how to grow a great cabbage. After glamour cabbages like the sugarloaves are all finished, there's always some dense red cabbages right at the end of the season that require a different method of cookery to really shine. So I came up with this cabbage schnitzel, where you braise the cabbage in roast chicken stock, thyme, butter and anchovy, then crumb and deep-fry it, and serve it up with an addictive anchovy mayonnaise.

Serves 4

½ red cabbage
120 g (4½ oz) butter
4 anchovy fillets
150 ml (5 fl oz) brown chicken
    stock (see page 186)
2 garlic cloves
4 thyme sprigs
1 egg
50 ml (1¾ fl oz) milk
100 g (3½ oz) plain (all-purpose)
    flour
250 g (9 oz) panko crumbs
oil, for deep frying
1 bunch young radicchio or
    similar bitter leaf

Anchovy Mayonnaise
2 eggs
15 g (½ oz) dijon mustard
25 g (1 oz) anchovy fillets
1 tablespoon oyster sauce
1 tablespoon lemon juice,
    plus extra for seasoning
1 tablespoon apple-cider
    vinegar
½ tablespoon Worcestershire
    sauce
230 ml (8 fl oz) grapeseed oil

Preheat the oven to 180°C (350°F).

Clean off the outside leaves of the cabbage and season them with salt and pepper. In a Dutch oven or large saucepan with a lid, let the butter melt over a low heat. Add the cabbage, cut side down, and let it cook for a few minutes, then add the anchovies, chicken stock, garlic and thyme. Cover and bring to the boil, then roast in the oven until fully cooked, about 40 minutes. Drain the cabbage, reserving the cooking juices, and chill overnight in the fridge, being careful to keep its original form as much as possible. Reduce the cooking juices by two thirds and reserve for dressing.

The next day, cut the cabbage into four wedges. Gently whisk the egg and milk together to form an egg wash. Dredge the cabbage segments through the flour, keeping them whole, then the egg wash, then the panko crumbs. Arrange on a tray lined with baking paper and chill until needed.

For the anchovy mayonnaise, combine the eggs, mustard, anchovies, oyster sauce, lemon juice, apple-cider vinegar and Worcestershire sauce in a blender and whizz until smooth. With the blender running, slowly drizzle in the oil a little at a time, making sure each addition is completely blended before adding any more. The sauce will thicken and lighten as you add the oil. At the end, it should be thick, shiny and fully emulsified.

Preheat a deep fryer or pot full of oil to 170°C (340°F). Deep fry the cabbage until golden on the outside and hot in the centre. Drain each wedge, then season with salt and some lemon juice. Carefully cut each wedge in two.

Arrange the cut wedges on plates with a pool of anchovy mayonnaise and the bitter leaves. Warm up and spoon over the cooking juices from the day before.

Annette's Tomatoes and Peaches with Honey Vinegar and Burrata Curds

While Tasmania seems like an odd place to be growing tomatoes, it's here that I've had some of the best tomatoes of my life. One of my friends put me onto a grower in the north, Annette, who hosts a once-a-year tomato festival. She sends the tomatoes out, all at exactly the same stage of ripeness, in colour-coded boxes, and grows more than 100 varieties including reisetomate and the best purple tomatillos I've ever had. It's made me understand the beauty of the tomato salad.

Serves 4

800 g (1 lb 12 oz) mixed
    heirloom tomatoes
1 teaspoon sea salt
80 ml (2½ fl oz/⅓ cup) Honey
    vinegar (page 227)
2 ripe peaches (optional)
80 ml (2½ fl oz/⅓ cup) olive oil
1 bunch fresh herbs of your
    choice (basil, mint, lemon
    verbena, whatever you like)

Burrata Curds

2 litres (68 fl oz/8 cups)
    unhomogenised milk
½ teaspoon citric acid dissolved
    in 60 ml (2 fl oz/¼ cup) water
7.5 ml (¼ fl oz) rennet mixed
    into 60 ml (2 fl oz/¼ cup)
    water
150 g (5½ oz) crème fraîche

For the burrata curds, pour the milk into a stainless-steel saucepan, add the citric acid dissolved in water and stir gently. Cook over a low heat, stirring very slowly, until the temperature comes up to 28°C (82°F). Add the rennet mixed with water and stir for another 10 seconds. Remove from the heat, cover and let it set for 15 minutes. Test the curds for a clean break by making a vertical cut into them with a palette knife, then lifting them up to see how clean the cut is. Cut into 5 cm (2 in) squares. Put back on the heat and slowly agitate with your hand, breaking up any large pieces until they reach 40°C (104°F). If you prefer the curds slightly drier, you can cook them out to 48°C (118°F) instead. Take them off the heat and let cool.

Once cool, drain the curds in a colander for 1 hour, then fold them with the crème fraîche and some salt to taste. Be very gentle so as not to overwork and whip the cream – it should look something like the inside of a ball of burrata. Keep in the fridge until needed.

Wash, core and slice the tomatoes, then put them in a bowl and season with the salt and honey vinegar. Let sit for 20 minutes. If using, remove the peach flesh from their kernels and cut into wedges, adding them and the olive oil to the bowl.

Spoon the cheese curds into a flat-bottomed bowl or onto a plate, then build the salad on top. Pour over some of the tomato juices and scatter with herbs.

Fresh Ricotta with Bottarga, Peas, Broad Beans and Asparagus

These are all young, green spring vegetables brought together in a cold salad with a salty bottarga vinaigrette and some homemade ricotta. After long, cold winters in Tassie, I like to celebrate spring and its plethora of vegetables as much as possible.

Serves 2–3

80 g (2¾ oz) fresh podded peas
100 g (3½ oz) podded
   broad beans
70 g (2½ oz) sugar-snap peas
1 bunch asparagus
1 bunch broad bean leaves
bottarga (salted, cured mullet
   roe), to serve

Ricotta

1 litre (34 fl oz/4 cups) milk
125 ml (4 fl oz) cream
1 teaspoon salt
40 ml (1¼ fl oz) white vinegar

Vinaigrette

50 ml (1¾ fl oz) olive oil
1 tablespoon brown rice mirin
½ tablespoon colatura* or
   good-quality fish sauce
juice of 1 lemon
15 g (½ oz) bottarga

For the ricotta, add the milk, cream and salt to a saucepan, stir to combine and bring up to 90°C (190°F) over a low heat. Add the vinegar, stir and leave to sit for 1 hour. Scoop into an 8 cm (3¼ in) cheese mould and leave to drain.

For the vinaigrette, combine all the liquids in a bowl and whisk, then microplane in the bottarga.

Bring a pot of salted water to the boil and blanch the vegetables, one at a time, for 30 seconds–1 minute, refreshing them in ice water immediately afterwards. Drain the vegetables. Cut the asparagus into rondelles (flat rounds), leaving the tips whole. Test the broad beans to see if they need to be double podded. Otherwise, leave the shells on.

Toss the vegetables with the vinaigrette and the broad bean leaves and serve alongside the ricotta turned out of the mould. Grate some more bottarga over the top to serve.

*Colatura is an amber-coloured fish sauce made from anchovies.

Salt-baked Beetroot with Macadamia and Mulberry

Salt-baked Beetroot with Macadamia and Mulberry

This is a simple, but results-driven way of cooking root vegetables. Salt baking a beetroot really adds to its sweet earthiness – so much so that one or two condiments is all you need to turn it into a dish. This technique works well with celeriac too.

Serves 4

3 medium golden beetroot (beets)

3 medium red beetroot (beets)

700 g (1 lb 9 oz) fine salt

75 g (2¾ oz, or about 3) egg whites

150 g (5½ oz) raw macadamia nuts

160 ml (5½ fl oz) water

juice of ½ lemon

1 garlic clove

100 ml (3½ fl oz) olive oil

8 mulberries, cut in half, to serve

40 ml (1¼ fl oz) Mulberry shrub (page 226) or good-quality sherry vinegar, to serve

20 tarragon leaves, to serve

bottarga (salted, cured mullet roe), to serve (optional)

Preheat the oven to 200°C (400°F). Line a tray with baking paper, then trim the tops off the beetroot, being careful to leave 1–2 cm (½–¾ in) of stalk. Arrange on the tray.

Combine the salt and egg white and mix until completely combined. Mould the mixture around each beetroot and bake for about 50 minutes, or until a skewer inserted into the middle meets no resistance.

In a blender, combine the macadamias, water and lemon juice, then microplane in the garlic. Blend on high for 5 minutes until as smooth as possible. With the blender running, pour in 40 ml (1¼ fl oz) oil and let it emulsify. Season with salt and set side.

Leave the beetroot to cool down slightly. While still warm, break the salt away and peel the beetroot. Discard the peels, stalks and salt. Cut the beetroots crossways into ½ cm (¼ in) slices. There's no need to season them with salt.

Spoon the macadamia sauce over a plate. Fan out the beetroot slices on top, alternating colours.

Top with the mulberries and spoon over the shrub, remaining oil and tarragon leaves and grate over some bottarga, if desired.

How To Poach a Rooster

This is my go-to chicken recipe, adapted from the first time I learned to stock-poach a chicken back when I worked at Quay. It was a revelation. It's taken on new significance for me since moving to Tasmania and starting to keep animals. What started as two chickens I was keeping for eggs turned into forty-five chickens with innumerable unruly roosters, and so I've had to learn to cull and cook with them. The broth this recipe produces is one of my favourite meal building blocks. I often add some soba noodles and poach a few mushrooms in it to create another dinner.

Serves 4

4 litres (135 fl oz/16 cups) water
160 ml (5½ fl oz) light
    soy sauce
50 ml (1¾ fl oz) mirin
50 ml (1¾ fl oz) shaoxing
    (Chinese rice wine),
      or substitute with sake or
      dry sherry
8 slices fresh ginger
½ garlic bulb
15 cm (6 in) dried seaweed
5 dried mushrooms
2 spring onions (scallions),
    quartered
1 rooster or chicken*

Combine all ingredients except the rooster in a stock pot and bring to a simmer. Check for seasoning and balance of flavours. Add the rooster, making sure to fully submerge it. Bring back to a simmer, then cover and take immediately off the heat. Leave to cool to room temperature, covered, then remove the bird from the stock. At this point I joint the bird and take the breasts off, then slice them and separate the leg into the thigh and drumstick. Gently warm the chicken in the broth to eat warm or have it cold, whole or picked down for a salad. Some of my favourite condiments to go along with it are pickled garlic cucumbers, poached shiitake mushrooms and a bit of lightly toasted sesame oil.

*To prepare a rooster after I have dispatched it, I heat a large pot of water to 65°C (150°F), then dunk and twist the bird in the pot of water for approximately 1 minute. This is just to facilitate plucking, but not to scald the skin or cook the meat. Then, on a flat surface, lie the bird down and pluck. After plucking, using a very sharp knife, remove the windpipe and crop. Gut the chicken, keeping the heart, liver and gizzard. I give the interior a small wash, then chill down in a refrigerator to cool and air dry. I age chicken for 5 days before cooking, but that is a personal matter of taste.

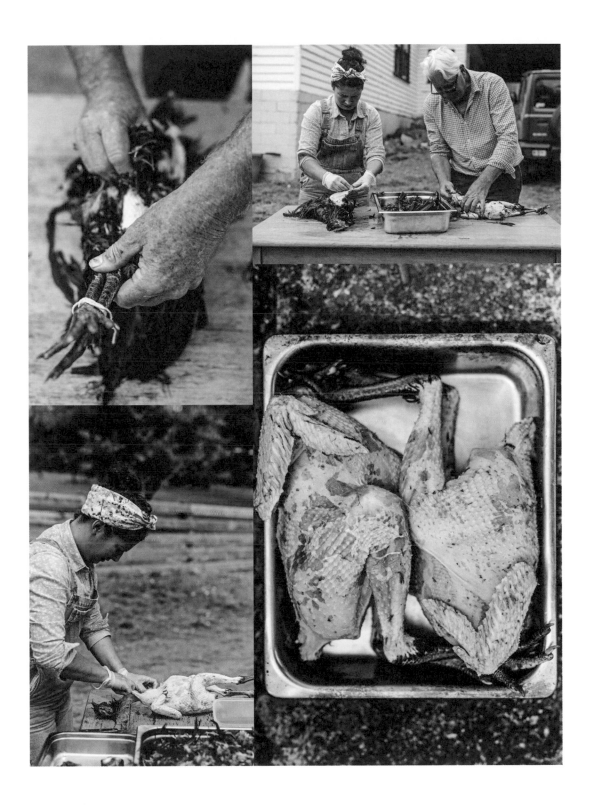

An emotional day learning how to kill roosters,
but a necessary part of country life – luckily, there are
friends in the community happy to show Analiese how

Wood-grilled Zucchini and Squash with Satsivi

Satsivi is a supremely savoury Georgian walnut paste traditionally served cold with vegetables and chicken. It was a bit of a revelation for me the first time I tried it. When I have it in the house I eat it on everything, including toast. This is my very non-traditional take on how to make it! I've paired it here with some late summer produce. I love to grill zucchini and squash over coals until they're silky and a bit smoky, then toss them with fresh herbs and vinegar as a warm salad.

Serves 4

8 golden squash
2 zucchini (courgettes)
olive oil, for brushing
1 tablespoon apple-cider
    vinegar
¼ bunch mint leaves, chopped
ricotta salata, to serve

Satsivi
250 g (9 oz) walnuts
2 tablespoons olive oil
1 onion, finely diced
2 garlic cloves, sliced
45 g (1½ oz) butter
½ teaspoon sweet smoked
    paprika
½ teaspoon za'atar
⅛ teaspoon ground cinnamon
¼ teaspoon ground fenugreek
⅛ teaspoon ground chilli
    (or to taste)
200 ml (7 fl oz) water
2 teaspoons pomegranate
    molasses
¼ bunch lovage or parsley,
    leaves picked
juice of 1 lemon

For the satsivi, grind the walnuts in a food processor until very fine. In a medium saucepan, add the olive oil and fry the onion and garlic gently until completely soft and sweet, or about 10 minutes. Add the walnuts and butter and toast everything together. Add the spices, water, molasses and lovage and cook, stirring, for 10 minutes. It should emulsify into a chunky sauce. Add the lemon juice, season with some salt and set aside.

Wash the squash and zucchini, brush with some olive oil and season with salt and pepper. Chargrill until very coloured on top and just cooked through. If you don't have the ability to chargrill you can pan-fry or grill (broil) them in your oven.

Cut the zucchini roughly and arrange in a bowl. Season with some sea salt, the apple-cider vinegar and mint leaves, then toss it all together. Serve warm alongside the walnut satsivi and with some shaved ricotta salata on top.

Pan-fried Flounder with Dill Pickles and Miso

One night, at about two in the morning, I found myself in a bay off Bruny Island, waist-high in freezing water with a fish spear and a torch, following a local in his search for flounder. After about an hour of wandering in the pitch-black dark, searching the bottom of the ocean for irregularities, we found them: two greenbacks. It may be the coldest I've ever been in my life. The next day, my partner Nick made me this dish with miso and dill pickles in a split beurre noisette sauce poured over pan-fried flounder, and all my memories of being icy cold ceased to matter.

Serves 2

1 tablespoon olive oil
1 (approximately 400–500 g/ 14 oz–1 lb 2 oz) plate-sized flounder, gutted and skin patted dry
110 g (4 oz) butter
50 g (1¾ oz) Chickpea miso (page 220) or slightly sweet miso
100 g (3½ oz) dill pickles, diced into ½ cm (¼ in) cubes
juice of 1 lemon
¼ bunch dill, finely chopped
¼ bunch chives, finely chopped
¼ bunch parsley, finely chopped
¼ bunch coriander (cilantro), finely chopped

Heat the olive oil until just before smoking point in a 30 cm (12 in) non-stick or seasoned cast-iron frying pan. Season the flounder, then lay it in the pan dark skin side down. Pan fry for 3 minutes, then turn carefully with a spatula and cook for another 2–3 minutes, or until just done. To test this, I often use a metal cake tester to check for resistance at the bone: the more cooked the fish is, the less resistance there will be. Take the fish out to rest, adding the butter to the same pan. When it foams, add in the miso and cook, stirring continuously. After about 2 minutes, add the dill pickles, cooking for another minute.

Turn off the heat and add the lemon juice and herbs. Season with a little salt to taste and spoon liberally over the flounder.

One of the experiences of living in Tasmania has
been learning to hunt and cook with wallaby

Wallaby Tartare with Beetroot, Radicchio and Pepperberry

Prior to moving to Tasmania, I had never eaten wallaby. Then one day, on a jaunt to Bruny Island, a friend bought me a wallaby rendang pie from the local store. A chance meeting with a wallaby hunter through some local fishermen followed, and before I knew it, I was at Bruny Island Game breaking down wallabies with Richard, the owner. He treats them with the utmost respect – the same way game is treated in Europe. Wallaby has been a food source for Aboriginal Tasmanians for thousands of years and, besides being delicious, it is an ethically responsible choice. I enjoy eating it raw in a tartare or sealed at a high temperature and served rare. It is very lean, so I tend to follow the same methods with it that I would to cook venison.

Serves 2

400 g (14 oz, or 1 large) purple beetroot (beets)
60 ml (2 fl oz/¼ cup) Blackcurrant shrub (page 226), or 40 ml (1¼ fl oz) red-wine vinegar or 20 g (¾ oz) honey
3 tablespoons olive oil
130 g (4½ oz) diced wallaby topside per person (you can also try beef or venison)
10 g (¼ oz) chives, chopped
10 g (¼ oz) shallot, chopped
pinch of ground pepperberry
15 g (½ oz) puffed wild rice
½ radicchio, to serve
3 cm (1¼ in) horseradish root, to serve

Trim the leaves off the beetroot. Place in a medium saucepan, cover with water and simmer until soft, about 40 minutes.

Drain the beetroot, discard the water and peel by hand, then cut into roughly 3 cm (1¼ in) cubes. In a clean pan, combine the beetroot with the shrub, salt to taste and 2 tablespoons olive oil and cook out on a low heat until the vinegar is reduced and glossy, about 10 minutes. Transfer to a blender and purée on high for 4 minutes. Cool and set aside. This recipe will make slightly more than you need, but any less and it wouldn't purée properly.

Trim any sinew from the wallaby and dice it into ½ cm (¼ in) cubes. Mix with the chives, shallot, remaining olive oil, pepperberry and wild rice and season to taste. Serve with the radicchio leaves and the beetroot purée, and microplane some fresh horseradish over the top.

Dry-aged Carpaccio of Dairy Cow with Pickled and Roasted Walnuts

One day I had a chance meeting with a dairy farmer when I was in search of milk. It led to a conversation about cooking retired dairy cows in high-end restaurants. This happened often when I lived in Spain, as opposed to them being sold for pet food as they often are in Australia. Fast-forward a year and a bit and farmer Ben from Old Cow Co had set up a cool room and dry-ageing facility and started selling his retired cows as beef. This is a dish I came up with for Franklin to showcase the meat's cheesy, nutty flavour.

Serves 2

120 g (4½ oz) dry-aged dairy cow, beef sirloin or rib eye
olive oil, for brushing
30 g (1 oz) walnuts, roasted and chopped
50 g (1¾ oz) Pickled walnut dressing (see below)
30 g (1 oz) ricotta salata, microplaned

Pickled Walnut Dressing
175 g (6 oz) pickled walnuts (preferably pickled in malt vinegar)
100 ml (3½ fl oz) olive oil
½ bunch chives

To make the dressing, drain the pickled walnuts, reserving the pickling liquid, and dice them into small cubes. Combine the olive oil, walnuts, malt vinegar and chives. Season with sea salt to taste.

Cut the beef into 3 cm (1¼ in) pieces. Lightly brush two sheets of baking paper with olive oil and place the beef between them. Using a mallet, bash the carpaccio to the desired thickness, approximately 3 mm (⅛ in). Remove one piece of paper and invert the beef onto a serving plate. Carefully peel off the other paper. Dress with the roasted walnuts, walnut dressing, ricotta salata and some flaky sea salt.

Roger's Gougères

These cheesy choux pastry puffs are one of my great loves of French patisserie and are surprisingly easy to make at home. This particular recipe is based off one from some Tasmanian friends, Roger and Sue, who host magical afternoons in the garden with champagne and gougères fresh from the oven. I mean, it probably helps that they're French wine importers and never short of a kilo or two of aged Comté. This recipe has stood me in good stead over the years. I've made these cheesy choux puffs at many events and at my wine bar, with Tasmanian cheddar at Franklin and with anchovies at wine fairs. The only tricky part is the baking!

Makes 30 gougères

220 ml (7½ fl oz) water
110 g (4 oz) butter
1 teaspoon salt
115 g (4 oz) plain (all-purpose) flour, sifted
180 g (6½ oz) egg, beaten
70 g (2½ oz) Pyengana cheddar (or Comté), finely grated, plus extra for sprinkling on top

Preheat the oven to 200°C (400°F).

In a large pot, bring the water, butter and salt to a slow simmer over a low heat. Add the flour. Using a spatula, cook on a low heat for 2–3 minutes, or until the mixture pulls away from the sides of the pan and forms a ball.

Transfer to a stand mixer with the paddle attachment and mix slowly for about 2 minutes, letting the mixture cool down slightly so as not to cook the egg. Add the egg a little at a time until fully incorporated, then the cheese. Cover with plastic wrap to keep a skin from forming and leave to cool.

Line a baking tray with baking paper and either spoon out or pipe the mixture in small rounds, leaving 4 cm (1½ in) in between each gougère to allow for spreading. Sprinkle the tops with the extra grated cheese. For gougères about 5 cm (2 in), they normally take 15 minutes to cook, but you can judge for yourself by checking their rise and colour: they should be golden and highly risen. They're best eaten right away, fresh from the oven, but they do reheat quite well too.

Jerusalem Artichoke Ice Cream with Hot Chocolate Malt

Jerusalem artichokes are good for a lot of things, but they make GREAT ice cream. This recipe continues my tradition of making winter desserts out of vegetables because that's what we have around at that time of year at the bottom of the world. This creamy j-choke ice cream is spiked with hot chocolate malt sauce, which I would generally put in a siphon at Franklin, but it is just as great poured over straight, like a hot, thick Milo.

Serves 4–6

250 g (9 oz) Jerusalem
　artichokes
375 ml (12½ fl oz) cream
375 ml (12½ fl oz/1½ cups) milk
100 g (3½ oz) sugar
6 egg yolks

Hot Malt Sauce

45 ml (1½ fl oz) water, plus
　1 tablespoon extra
65 g (2¼ oz) sugar
500 ml (17 fl oz) cream
65 g (2¼ oz) milk chocolate
75 g (2¾ oz) liquid malt extract
65 g (2¼ oz) freeze-dried
　medium malt extract
1 teaspoon cornflour
　(cornstarch)

Preheat the oven to 160°C (320°F).

Wash the artichokes, arrange them in a roasting tin and roast, without oil and uncovered, in the oven for about 40 minutes until completely soft.

In a saucepan, warm the cream and artichokes over a low heat for about 4 minutes, then add to a blender and blend until smooth. There will be small pieces of skin left, but not to worry: you'll strain the mix later.

Combine the cream mixture and the milk in a saucepan and warm through gently over a low heat. In a bowl, whisk the sugar and egg yolks, then pour the hot cream over and whisk before pouring the mix into a clean saucepan or double boiler. Cook slowly, stirring constantly with a spatula, over a low heat, until the anglaise reaches 85°C (185°F); it will thicken slightly during this process. Pass it through a fine chinois (conical sieve/strainer) into a bowl and chill over ice before freezing. Freeze in an ice cream maker according to the manufacturer's instructions.

For the malt sauce, make a caramel with the sugar and water. Combine the 45 ml (1½ fl oz) water and the sugar in a saucepan, place on a medium heat and cook until the water has evaporated and the sugar is golden brown, or at a temperature of 160°C (320°F). I suggest you use a candy thermometer for this process. Pour in the cream and whisk until smooth. It's important to use a larger pot than you think you need for this process because when you 'break' the caramel with the cream, it will react violently. Add the chocolate and malt extracts and cook gently, stirring until smooth and silky. In a small bowl, mix the cornflour with 1 tablespoon water, then add to the pot and cook until slightly thickened, about 3 minutes. You can eat the sauce straight away or pour into a siphon and charge it with one nitrous oxide cartridge, shake to mix, discharge into a bowl and top with the ice cream.

Hasselback Jerusalem Artichokes with Coppa, Saltbush and Whipped Curd

This is a dish I would cook in a woodfired oven. Jerusalem artichokes cut hasselback style, then roasted, tossed with coppa (dry-cured pork), sunflower seeds and crispy saltbush sat on whipped curd and loaded with black pepper, garlic and fresh herbs. Essentially, it's a play on a baked potato.

Serves 2–4

50 saltbush leaves
500 g (1 lb 2 oz) Jerusalem artichokes
1 garlic bulb, plus 1 extra clove
40 ml (1¼ fl oz) grapeseed oil
250 g (9 oz) drained Goat's curd (page 230)
¼ bunch chives, finely chopped
¼ bunch garlic chives, finely chopped
¼ bunch dill, finely chopped
¼ bunch tarragon, finely chopped
40 g (1½ oz) fried sunflower seeds
10 slices coppa (you can also use prosciutto)
juice of 1 lemon

Preheat the oven to 180°C (350°F).

Arrange the saltbush leaves on a dry baking tray and bake until crispy, but not coloured; this will take about 30 minutes. Alternatively, you can deep-fry them at 160°C (320°F) until crispy, then drain and set aside.

Wash and scrub the artichokes to remove any grit. Holding an artichoke in one hand, cut it hasselback style, the same way you would a potato. Repeat with the rest of the artichokes. Put them in a cast-iron frying pan with the garlic bulb, oil and some sea salt. Roast until crispy on the outside and soft in the centre, about 1 hour. Once out, turn the oven down to 160°C (320°F).

In a bowl, mix the curd and herbs and season with sea salt and black pepper. Microplane in the clove of garlic and whip using a whisk until light and fluffy. Test the seasoning.

Toss the artichokes in a bowl with the sunflower seeds, coppa, saltbush leaves and lemon juice. Spread the mix out over a plate and serve with spoonfuls of curd.

Mulberry Clafoutis

Mulberry Clafoutis

Mulberry may be my favourite clafoutis, but I'm also partial to cherry, apricot, fig and rhubarb. In fact, pretty much any stone fruit or berry is great in this dessert. In countryside France it's often eaten cold and sliced like a tart, but at Franklin we baked them to order in the woodfired oven and sent them out hot, topped with cultured cream and honey. The cold version has become one of my favourite things to pack for a picnic, full of tart, jammy summer fruits.

Makes 1 clafoutis/Serves 6

100 g (3½ oz) sugar
60 g (2 oz, about 4) egg yolks
120 g (4½ oz) egg
250 ml (8½ fl oz) cream
70 g (2½ oz) almond meal
10 g (¼ oz) plain (all-purpose)
   flour, sifted
150 g (5½ oz) fresh mulberries
mascarpone, to serve (optional)
honeycomb, to serve (optional)

Preheat the oven to 180°C (350°F).

In a bowl, gently whisk the sugar, yolks and eggs without creating any foam. Add the cream and whisk to incorporate. Add the almond meal and flour and whisk gently until smooth.

Line a 20–25 cm (8–10 in) steel pan or tart dish with baking paper and pour in the batter. Drop the fruit sporadically on top and bake for approximately 40 minutes until golden on top and still slightly wobbly in the centre.

I've served it with local mascarpone and honeycomb, but it's equally great with ice cream, cream or just on its own.

Cherry Kernel Baked Panna Cotta with Fresh Cherries and Fig Leaf Granita

This variation on a traditional baked panna cotta came to me from an Italian friend's grandmother. I love the texture that comes from baking the custard with just egg whites at a low temperature: super silky and smooth, yet somehow lighter than a traditional custard. The flavour combination just happens to be several things that are in season during the Tasmanian summer, and they are really complementary flavours.

Makes 1 panna cotta/ Serves 4

50 g (1¾ oz) cherry kernels (pits)
500 ml (17 fl oz) cream
70 g (2½ oz) egg whites
40 g (1½ oz) caster (superfine) sugar
16 cherries

Fig Leaf Granita
250 ml (8½ fl oz/1 cup) water
100 g (3½ oz) sugar
½ vanilla bean
2 fig leaves, washed and stalks trimmed
250 ml (8½ fl oz/1 cup) apple juice, fresh and high quality

For the granita, combine the water, sugar and scraped vanilla bean and seeds in a saucepan and bring to a simmer. Finely chop the fig leaves and put them in a heatproof bowl. Pour the hot syrup over and leave to infuse until cool. Pass through a fine chinois (conical sieve/strainer), really pressing the leaves. If you like a lot of fig leaf flavour and want it really green, you can give it a quick buzz in a blender before passing it through. Add the apple juice and stir well. Freeze until solid, then scratch with a fork to create ice crystals.

Preheat the oven to 90°C (190°F).

Blend the cherry kernels until they resemble coarse crumbs, then add to a bowl with the cream and leave to infuse overnight. Strain the cream and discard the kernels. In a bowl, gently whisk the egg whites and sugar – not to foam, but just to break them up. Slowly whisk in the cream until just incorporated. Pass the mix through a fine chinois into an ovenproof dish.

Bake for 45 minutes, or until just set. It can also be steamed, covered, at the same temperature for 45 minutes if you have access to a steamer. Chill and leave to set, preferably overnight.

Halve the cherries and remove their pits, reserving them in the freezer for future use. With a large spoon, scoop out a portion of custard and place it in a bowl. Scatter over the cherries and top with freshly forked granita.

Chocolate and Liquorice Cake

Chocolate and Liquorice Cake

A strangely addictive cake with a decent amount of aniseed flavour, reminiscent of a chocolate bullet. When I served this at Franklin, I'd often find the staff post service in the washup area hunting for cake trimmings. It's a variation on a recipe I learned from Finnish chef Pasi Petanen, who uses it as the base for his carrot, yoghurt and liquorice dessert at Café Paci in Sydney. When I served this at Franklin, we would garnish it with wild fennel ice cream and some finely shaved fennel bulb macerated in a vermouth and absinthe sugar syrup.

Makes 1 cake/Serves 4–6

150 g (5½ oz) caster (superfine) sugar
130 g (4½ oz) plain (all-purpose) flour
40 g (1½ oz) brown sugar
7 g (¼ oz) baking powder
3 g (¹⁄₁₀ oz) bicarbonate of soda (baking soda)
1 g (¹⁄₂₈ oz) salt
1 g (¹⁄₂₈ oz) powdered star anise
100 ml (3½ fl oz) molasses
100 ml (3½ fl oz) vegetable oil
100 ml (3½ fl oz) orange juice
90 ml (3 fl oz) Liquorice water (see below)
1 egg
1 egg yolk

Liquorice Water
1 bag hard aniseed candy such as humbugs
500 ml (17 fl oz/2 cups) water

Chocolate Liquorice Ganache
260 g (9 oz) soft organic liquorice
400 ml (13½ fl oz) water
100 g (3½ oz) 70% dark chocolate, broken up into pieces

Garnish (optional)
80 g (2¾ oz) sugar
80 ml (2½ fl oz/⅓ cup) water
30 ml (1 fl oz) white vermouth
½ fennel bulb
wild fennel fronds, to garnish

For the liquorice water, bring the humbugs and water to a simmer over a gentle heat, stirring occasionally, until the candy is completely melted. Set aside in the fridge.

For the chocolate liquorice ganache, finely chop the liquorice and combine with the water in a saucepan on the stove. Melt over a low heat, stirring often. When nearly melted, transfer to a blender and blend until smooth. While the mixture is still hot, add the chocolate and mix until a silky ganache forms. Pour into a container and set aside.

Preheat the oven to 175°C (340°F).

In a bowl, sift the dry ingredients. In a separate bowl, whisk the wet ingredients and eggs, then pour them into the dry and mix gently with your whisk until smooth. Pour the batter into a lined 24 × 15 cm (9½ × 6 in) stainless-steel or aluminium cake tin. Bake for 45 minutes, or until a skewer inserted comes out clean. Cool in the tin before turning out.

To glaze the cake, trim the top with a serrated knife to make it flat, then place on a cake rack set over a tray. Warm the ganache gently in a saucepan, stirring all the time. Pour over the cake, making sure it covers the whole surface, then place in the fridge to set. Once set, trim away all the edges to make it nice and square so you can see the delineation of cake and ganache.

For the garnish, if making, combine the sugar and water in a small saucepan and heat until the sugar is dissolved, then take off the heat to cool. When cool, add the vermouth. To prepare the fennel, peel the outside with a peeler, then shave it thinly on a mandoline. Macerate the fennel in the vermouth syrup and keep in the fridge to serve cold, garnished with fennel fronds, if desired.

Ricotta and Leatherwood Honey Ice Cream with Fresh Goat's Curd and Mandarin Granita

A winter dessert, but one that holds the taste of summer. Super-rich ricotta ice cream flavoured only with leatherwood honey, offset by some silky, tangy, just-set goat's curd and mandarin ice crystals. An odd combination, but as with so many dishes, one where the whole is definitely greater than the sum of its parts.

Serves 4–6

250 ml (8½ fl oz) cream
100 g (3½ oz) caster (superfine) sugar
80 g (2¾ oz) leatherwood honey
5 egg yolks
500 g (1 lb 2 oz) ricotta (page 180)
1 dessert spoon fresh Goat's curd (page 230), to serve

Mandarin Granita
700 ml (23½ fl oz) mandarin juice
100 g (3½ oz) granulated sugar
50 ml (1¾ fl oz) yuzushu*, or any citrus-based liqueur

In a medium saucepan, heat the cream to just under a boil. In a bowl, whisk the sugar, honey and egg yolks. Pour in the hot cream and whisk gently to combine. Return to the pan and cook out on a low heat, stirring constantly with a spatula, until the mixture reaches 85°C (185°F), then cool immediately in an ice bath. Alternatively, you can cook the anglaise out in a double boiler. Once cold, pour the mix into a blender, add the ricotta and process until smooth. Freeze in an ice cream maker according to the manufacturer's instructions. The ricotta makes this ice cream base very thick and custardlike.

For the granita, heat 100 ml (3½ fl oz) of the mandarin juice and the sugar in a small saucepan over a low heat, just enough to dissolve it. Cool down, then add the rest of the mandarin juice and yuzushu. Freeze in a tray until solid, then scratch with a fork to fluff up some ice crystals.

To serve, put a spoonful of ice cream in the bottom of a cold bowl, make a divot in the centre and add the goat's curd, then top with freshly forked granita.

*A sweetened combination of sake and yuzu juice.

FERMENTS

Fermented Shiitake Mushrooms

These mushrooms are one of my favourite finds from those moments where you look at a vegetable and think 'I wonder if ...'. The fermentation makes them soft, salty and delicious as a condiment or pickle. I also heat them up and use them as a garnish for meat-based dishes. This basic lacto fermentation recipe for brining is best used on whole, smaller vegetables.

Makes 500 g (1 lb 2 oz)

500 g (1 lb 2 oz) shiitake mushrooms, stems removed
10 g (¼ oz) sea salt
1 litre (34 fl oz/4 cups) 2% salt brine

In a bowl, toss together the mushrooms and salt. Pack the mushrooms into a crock or another non-metallic fermentation vessel. Pour the brine over the mushrooms until just covered and weigh them down with a weight or small plate to keep them under the brine's surface. Cover and store in a cool, dark place. From day five I start checking the mushrooms every day, using a clean utensil. Once the fermentation has reached your desired level, decant to a container and store in the fridge to slow down fermentation. The brine can be used again on your next batch of mushrooms, which will ferment faster because of it.

Chickpea Miso

I hesitate to call this miso because it's an untraditional blend of chickpeas, koji and salt. But when made using chickpeas in the miso process, it becomes a delicious paste with equal amounts of sweetness and umami. I stick a spoonful in most of my soups, risottos, dips ... just about anything, actually!

Makes approx. 2.8 kg (6 lb)

1 kg (2 lb 3 oz) dried chickpeas
1 tablespoon premade miso
300 g (10½ oz) sea salt
1 kg (2 lb 3 oz) white rice koji

Soak the chickpeas in cold water for 12 hours. Drain and put the chickpeas in a saucepan, then cover with water. Bring to the boil, then turn the heat down to a simmer. Skim off any scum that rises to the surface while cooking; don't season the chickpeas at this stage. Cook until you can easily crush a chickpea between your fingers, then drain, reserving the cooking liquid.

Mash the cooked chickpeas either by hand or in a stand mixer fitted with the paddle attachment. Mix the premade miso with 125 ml (4 fl oz/½ cup) water and add it to the mix. Add about 80 per cent of the salt and mix well. Once the temperature of the mix is below 45°C (113°F) you can add the koji; if it's too hot it will kill some of the spores. Mix everything well. It should be a very thick paste, not dry and crumbly. If the mix feels dry, I add some of the chickpea cooking water and mix it through.

Pack the mix into a fermentation crock, leaving no air pockets. Smooth the surface and spread the remaining salt over the top to inhibit mould growth. Cover with paper and a weight (I use the ceramic ones that came with my crock). Cover and store in a cool, dark place. I find this miso takes about three months to get to the stage I enjoy, with a balance between sweetness and umami. At this stage I clean any mould growth off the top and pack the miso into containers to keep in the fridge.

Kefir Cream

I often make kefir cream as a sour cream or crème fraîche substitute, or to turn into cultured butter. At Franklin I used a lot less mesophilic starter cultures this way, and I genuinely enjoy looking after my kefir grains or my 'kefir family', as I call them.

Makes 2 litres (68 fl oz)

2 litres (68 fl oz) cream
90 ml (3 fl oz) inoculated kefir milk

In a large saucepan, set the cream over a low heat and bring it up to 30°C (86°F). Pour it into a container with a lid. Add the inoculated milk and stir to combine. Leave for 24–48 hours at room temperature. I keep the cream out until it has mostly set with a pronounced jiggle in the centre, then refrigerate it. It should have a lactic, slightly sour smell, but it should not be yeasty. Once cooled, the cream is ready to use or can be churned into butter.

Kefir Butter

I have a friend in Tasmania who makes her own kefir butter. I've always been inordinately impressed by this: to go to someone's home and see a pat of yellow, tangy kefir butter complete with large salt crystals for your bread. When I have the time, I now do the same, roll it in baking paper and keep it in the fridge. It's a great use of leftover cream as well. If I'm planning on using it for cooking, I don't add any salt and just pack it into a container for use.

Makes 450 g (1 lb)

1 litre (34 fl oz) Kefir cream (see on left)
250 ml (8½ fl oz/1 cup) ice water
sea salt

Pour the cream into the bowl of a stand mixer fitted with the whisk attachment, or a food processor. Process on medium speed until the butter fat separates from the buttermilk into yellow curds, about 5–10 minutes. Strain the mixture through a sieve into a bowl to collect the butter and buttermilk.

Let the butter drip for several minutes. Then, using your hands, gather it into a ball and squeeze the buttermilk out. Keep the buttermilk in the fridge for future recipes.

Transfer the butter to a clean bowl and add the ice water. Using a spatula, fold the butter over on itself repeatedly to clean it of residual buttermilk. Discard the water. Repeat this process until the liquid is clear.

Move the butter onto a tea towel (dish towel) and pat it dry. Sprinkle with sea salt and knead it in. Place half the butter in the centre of a piece of baking paper and roll it into a log. Fold the ends of the paper down. Repeat the process with the other half. Keep in the fridge.

Kefir Butter

225

Kombucha

Kombucha is a sweet fermented tea that utilises SCOBY, or a symbiotic community of bacteria and yeasts, for fermentation. It is delicious and has the added benefit of being good for your digestive and immune systems. I fell down the kombucha rabbit hole when I became lactose intolerant and started having innumerable gut issues, and I really do feel it has helped my digestive system. This is a basic recipe for a batch kombucha, which is the best place to start. From here you can diversify to the continuous method or to secondary fermentations, but it's good to master the basics first!

Makes 5 litres (170 fl oz)

5 litres (170 fl oz) water
25 g (1 oz) tea (I like to use English breakfast to start)
370 g (13 oz) raw granulated sugar
500 ml (17 fl oz/2 cups) kombucha from your last batch, or use a ready-made one to start
1 SCOBY

In a large pot, bring your water to the boil. Take off the heat and add the tea and sugar and leave to infuse and cool. Once cool, pour the liquid through a strainer into a jar or crock to ferment. This is important, as you should never add your SCOBY to liquid that is above 35°C (95°F). Add the premade kombucha and stir to combine. Add the SCOBY, cover with muslin (cheesecloth) and leave somewhere out of direct sunlight. I check on my kombucha every day, but start tasting it from day five onwards to find the sweet spot between acidity and sweetness, flavour-wise. Once you have hit your desired level of acidity, remove the SCOBY, put it in a separate container (I place mine in a 'SCOBY hotel' – a jar containing the SCOBY covered in kombucha), and refrigerate the kombucha to slow down any more fermentation. You can bottle it, but I tend to keep it in a crock with a tap so I can enjoy it straight from the fridge.

Fruit-based Shrubs

A shrub is essentially a drinking vinegar that combines fruit, sugar and vinegar. Making shrubs is a technique I acquired from working alongside cocktail bartenders, who make them as a base for cocktails or to top with soda water as a kind of natural soft drink. I've adapted this recipe to cut out the sugar and just use unpasteurised honey. I always use unpasteurised apple-cider vinegar too. Shrubs have become the basis of many of my dressings for things from vegetables to raw fish. I make them in summer and autumn, when fruits are plentiful, which leaves me with a large selection of flavours come winter.

Makes 1 litre (34 fl oz/4 cups)

1 kg (2 lb 3 oz) ripe fruit
1 kg (2 lb 3 oz) unpasteurised honey
1 litre (34 fl oz/4 cups) unpasteurised apple-cider vinegar

Combine whole, clean fruit with the honey and vinegar and store in an non-reactive bottle or container with a lid. I stir it every day for a week to make sure the honey is dissolved and not settling. After 3 weeks, strain out the fruit and refrigerate the shrub. I keep the fruit solids refrigerated, too, and use them in sauces and condiments where you would use umeboshi or other pickled components.

Some of the flavours I always return to are:

• Blackcurrant
• Apricot
• Cherry
• Mulberry
• Plum

Honey Vinegar

I make this version of honey or mead vinegar every year, especially considering Tasmania has such great single-flower honeys. It's a beautiful product that has become one of my pantry essentials. Every summer I douse tomatoes in it, deglaze pans with it, and use it anywhere you want a touch of sweetness, but also some acidity.

Makes 2.2 litres (76 fl oz) vinegar

1 kg (2 lb 3 oz) honey
800 ml (27 fl oz) live vinegar or unpasteurised apple-cider vinegar
250 ml (8½ fl oz/1 cup) water
250 ml (8½ fl oz/1 cup) rum
1 vinegar mother

Combine everything except the vinegar mother. Transfer to a demijohn or a suitable fermentation vessel. Add the vinegar mother, cover the mouth of the vessel with an airlock or cloth, and leave to ferment for two weeks. After that, check on it occasionally, waiting until it's acidic and floral with no trace of alcohol.

Garum

When I was doing research and development at a restaurant in Spain, one of my projects was to make fish sauce for the restaurant. At a salt level of 20 per cent, there is no water in the mix for harmful bacteria to grow in, therefore it is the safest level if you want to try and make garum yourself. Still, I would only try and make this if your fish scraps are impeccably fresh. The results are much better with oily fish such as mackerel, sardines or anchovies.

Makes approx. 1 litre (34 fl oz/4 cups)

1 kg (2 lb 3 oz) fish waste, bones, heads, guts (I like sardines)
200 g (7 oz) salt

Mix the fish waste and salt. Pack into a jar or ceramic crock and seal with a lid.

Store in a 50°C (120°F) fermentation chamber for 7 days, shaking the jar once a day (I use a dehydrator set to 50°C; you could also use a heat pad/cool box set-up, or look up suggestions on how to create fermentation chambers online).

Once finished (most solids should be broken down), strain through a coffee filter or muslin (cheesecloth), discard the solids and keep sealed in the fridge.

Lemon Verbena
Kombucha
18.4

Wakame Jam

Seaweed jam has fast become one of my favourite condiments after discovering it in Kyoto, made with kombu and used in dashi. I make my own version from wild-harvested wakame (an edible seaweed originating from Japan that is an invasive species down here in Tasmania). I prefer to make it from the fruiting base of the plant, also known as mekabu. Umami rich, sweet and salty, it's a great base for many sauces or just as something to throw on a grilled flounder.

Makes approx. 400 g (14 oz)

90 ml (3 fl oz) light soy sauce
110 ml (4 fl oz) mirin
850 ml (28½ fl oz) water
100 g (3½ oz) dried wakame (preferably mekabu)
40 g (1½ oz) raw (demerara) sugar

In a medium pot, combine the soy, mirin and water and bring to a simmer. Add the seaweed, making sure it is submerged, then take the pot off the heat and leave to rehydrate for 2 hours. Return the pot, covered, to a low heat and braise the seaweed slowly for 1½ hours, or until completely tender. Drain in a colander placed over a bowl (you want to reserve the braising liquid).

Finely chop or shred the wakame and return it to the pot. Add the braising liquid and sugar and cook for 30 minutes over a medium heat, stirring all the time. You want the liquid to reduce completely to form a thick, gelatinous, glossy sauce.

Take the pot off the stove, cool and keep covered in the fridge. If wanting to preserve it for a long time, you can vacuum pack it or process it in sealed jars.

Goat's Curd

There may not be anything as rewarding as making cheese. This is a recipe for a fresh, lactic acid–set goat's milk cheese. The more you drain it, the firmer and denser it will become. It's perfect for incorporating into dishes, desserts, or just enjoying on bread or with some fresh vegetables. Before making this, I always sterilise my equipment with boiling water.

Makes 500 g–1 kg (1 lb 2 oz–2 lb 3 oz), depending on drainage

2 litres (68 fl oz/8 cups) goat's milk
10 g (¼ oz) salt
⅛ teaspoon Flora Danica culture
2 drops rennet mixed with 1 tablespoon water

In a pot over a low heat, bring the milk up to 25°C (77°F). Take off the heat, add the salt and gently mix it through. Sprinkle in the culture and leave to hydrate for 5 minutes. Stir gently for a full 2 minutes. Add the rennet–water combination and stir gently for 2 minutes. Cover and keep at 22°C (71°F) for 8 hours or overnight.

When the milk has set to a white, soft curd with a layer of clear whey on top, it is ready. Put a strainer over a large bowl and line it with muslin (cheesecloth). Ladle the curd into the strainer and leave to drain until it's lost half its volume in whey.

Pack the curd into containers and keep in the fridge.

Acknowledgements

To Fay, Ina and Joy, the Chinese matriarchs of my family, who taught me to cook, to be resilient and how to test a winter melon with my pinky nail.

I am blessed to have friends I could not have done this without – to Bruce Kemp, Nick Stanton and Jo Barrett for allowing me to suck you into these pages.

To the whole Hobart family for taking me in as part of the community, teaching me the ways of life in Tasmania and being there through the ups and the downs.

Thank you to Jane Willson, Anna Collett, Adam Gibson, Hilary Burden and the team at Hardie Grant for putting up with me, taking a chance and educating me.

Index

Published in 2021 by Hardie Grant Books,
an imprint of Hardie Grant Publishing

Hardie Grant Books (Melbourne)
Building 1, 658 Church Street
Richmond, Victoria 3121

Hardie Grant Books (London)
5th & 6th Floors
52–54 Southwark Street
London SE1 1UN

hardiegrantbooks.com

Hardie Grant acknowledges the Traditional Owners of the country on which we work, the
Wurundjeri people of the Kulin Nation and the Gadigal people of the Eora Nation, and recognises
their continuing connection to the land, waters and culture. We pay our respects to their Elders
past, present and emerging.

A catalogue record for this
book is available from the
National Library of Australia

How Wild Things Are
ISBN 978 1 74379 602 3

10 9 8 7 6 5 4 3 2 1

Publishing Director: Jane Willson
Project Editor: Anna Collett
Editor: Kate J Armstrong
Writer: Hilary Burden
Design Manager: Jessica Lowe/Mietta Yans
Designer/Illustrator: Daniel New
Photographer: Adam Gibson
Stylist: Lee Blaylock
Production Manager: Todd Rechner

Colour reproduction by Splitting Image Colour Studio
Printed in China by Leo Paper Products LTD.

The paper this book is printed on is from FSC®-
certified forests and other sources. FSC® promotes environmentally responsible, socially beneficial
and economically viable management of the world's forests.

The oven temperatures in this book are for conventional ovens.
If using a fan-forced oven, reduce the temperature by 20°C (70°F).
This book uses 250 ml (8½ fl oz) cups and 20 ml (¾ fl oz) tablespoons.

This girl is a force to be reckoned with.

GORDON RAMSAY

Analiese is one of the next generation of Australian chefs to inspire and lead our food culture – her passion and talent truly stood out in the years she worked with me at Quay, and her unique style is the accumulation of her travels and life experiences.

PETER GILMORE, QUAY, SYDNEY

Analiese's cooking is a cross-pollination of her heritage, training and love of nature. It is soulful and joyful, balanced and nuanced with a complexity that can only come from someone who has lived, loved and thrown herself at life full throttle. If you want to know how to cook as a modern person who lives off the land, buy this book and relish it.

PALISA ANDERSON, BOON LUCK FARM, BYRON BAY